Paul Mace's Tools for Windows

Paul Mace's Tools for Windows

Paul Mace
Jeffrey Gordon Angus

RANDOM HOUSE
ELECTRONIC PUBLISHING

New York

Paul Mace's Tools for Windows

Copyright © 1994 by Paul Mace

Published in the United States by Random House, Inc., New York, and simultaneously in Canada by Random House of Canada, Limited.

Produced and composed by Parker-Fields Typesetters, Ltd.

Manufactured in the United States of America

First Edition

0   9   8   7   6   5   4   3   2   1

ISBN 0-679-79123-X

New York   Toronto   London   Sydney   Auckland

Contents

Introduction

In the years since its first release in 1985, I have installed new versions of Microsoft Windows on my computer at least once a year. Until the release of Windows 3.0, I always ended up throwing it off my machine in disgust. I mention this here to satisfy any concern you might have that I have not been skeptical about Windows. I am not one of the sycophantic mass that adores Windows for what it is *in principle*; I like what's good about it and dislike its weaknesses.

Under DOS, if you know the right command, you simply type it in, press Enter, and things happen; if you don't know the command, of course, you quickly end up feeling like a chimp. You can press keys all day and get nowhere. True, you can buy a book of incantations and initiate yourself into the mysteries of DOS, but it seems like a lot when all you want to do is write a letter. I remember thinking there oughta be a law against this sort of thing.

If DOS won't show its face, Windows goes the other way—it's got a million faces, and you can't make them go away or always tell which is the real Windows. It is, in many ways, like the TV game show *Concentration,* where you don't need to know much; you only need to find and remember the position of an item. In Windows, you need to know which program icon or menu item you want, then use the mouse or keyboard to bring it into view so you can "select" it. This can be fun, or at least a pleasant challenge—up to a point. I swear someone keeps moving things around when I'm not looking, because I often waste a lot of time looking for something where it isn't.

Still, I let Windows 3.0 stay on my machine, for two reasons: I was finally convinced that Windows was inevitable and had decided to develop software for it, and it was useful—that is, there were things I could do under Windows that I could not do under DOS. Specifically, there was hardware coming to market—graphics cards, scanners, printers—that offered dramatic improvement displaying graphical information at reasonable prices. The easiest way to integrate this hardware into my system was through Windows, for which everything had device drivers. The question was, could I live in both worlds, DOS and Windows, switching back and forth? That was a requirement I couldn't escape, for it was equally true that some things I expected in the way of software tools were not available for Windows or were pale imitations of the DOS equivalents.

Slowly, over the last two years, the situation has shifted. This book is the result, in part, of my desire to give up this fickle existence and embrace Windows completely. Which is really no more than I had wanted nearly ten years earlier when, having broken my typewriter, I sat before my first C:> prompt, making an idiot of myself.

That doesn't mean you can't make an idiot of yourself using Win 3.1 or feel like an ass when you have to pony up more and more dollars for utility software that makes Windows do what you thought it would do out of the box. Part of the disappointment with Windows and my irritation with Microsoft comes from believing Microsoft is a leading-edge software developer. Well, they *are* and they (mostly) *aren't*. Microsoft engineers and executives seem to adhere to the 80-20 rule. Knowing that the last 20 percent of what is technically achievable will soak up as much effort, time, and money as the first 80 percent, they stop short. Always and deliberately, in my opinion.

They believe, correctly, that other companies will supply the missing pieces. They can then decide, based on the marketplace reaction to other vendors' products, whether to ignore specific improvements, delay them, license the product (for a pittance), or add the feature to Windows. The last 20 percent of functionality is often damn hard to achieve, requiring insight and invention. And, once invented, it is trivial for other experts to see what it was they were missing and duplicate it or do something similar. Visionaries in this business are routinely stomped, chewed, and screwed by larger competitors, not to mention their own business partners and investors. There is a lot of money involved, and money, in large amounts, is surrounded by its own morality.

It is equally true, however, for the end user, that frustration and disappointment often result. After all, Windows doesn't carry a disclaimer on the package, "Complete satisfaction will require the purchase of $1000 worth of additional utilities."

This book acknowledges the need for such a disclaimer, but it also tries to act as a guidebook for the Windows user who's trying to get a pair of arms around what's missing and make some sensible choices between alternatives.

So, let's first take a look at Windows 3.1—where it succeeds and where it's deficient. Then we'll tackle the partial fulfillment of Bill Gates' dream, all those little (and not so little) desktop managers you can mix and match within Windows to cooperate in achieving your specific goals. Finally, we'll take a look at six Windows utilities that are included with this book.

SECTION 1

Windows 3.1

1

Windows 3.1 and Its Utilities

Overview

There is a new, clean, black-and-white look to the Windows 3.1 package—gone is the blue from the old days, when Microsoft identified its future with IBM. We're on our own now. The logo—the wavy window, trailing pixels—will be our eyeball code when shopping for Windows software. If we don't see it, our eye won't pause, no matter how clever the packaging or promises. We have passed the point where DOS offers something Windows does not—switching back and forth is a major irritant. After all these years, the solution is not to kick Windows off the disk, but rather to leave DOS and DOS applications behind for good!

Version 3.1. A modest increment. Microsoft has always been spartan in allocating version numbers to this product. Norton's at 7, WordPerfect's a solid 6. Admittedly, version numbers are measured with a rubber ruler, but there is a kind of ethic to it, that runs as follows: Major releases almost always look different. This is usually accompanied by promises like the one on the back of the Windows package: MAKES YOUR PC EASIER TO USE. This I interpret to mean that the company was taking a lot of heat for its last interface design and has taken another stab at it. Win 3.0 was a noticeable improvement on Win 2.0, and Microsoft has not monkeyed with the look and feel for this release. This is the way it will stay for a while, until the Apple copyright infringement suit is settled once and for all.

Major releases almost always include a truckload of new features. With Win 3.1 we get maybe a trunkload, with True Type scalable fonts. That means your Windows word processor or typesetting program can display and print a wider range of type sizes without the screen or final page looking like alphabet blocks.

Minor releases signify technical improvements. This is a cryptic way within the industry of signaling that most of the unfulfilled promises of the last major release have now been addressed. Win 3.1 is no exception.

Windows has always been notorious for falling over dead when you tried to do something simple, like switch from one application to another, or start a DOS application, or, well, when the room lighting wasn't just so, or you were hungry, or when there was an earthquake in Chile. Technically, we would say, "Windows is not robust," meaning there were too many ways an application or user could mortally wound it. Of course, the joy of any multitasking computer is to watch not one but several major pieces of work bite the dust in unison.

Win 3.0 was a major step forward for Windows, but there remained the dreaded UAE (unrecoverable application error). The computing equivalent of a stroke, it meant that some task had caused a processor fault and that Windows had detected it and stopped that application from executing. Unfortunately, it usually meant it had stopped every other task as well. If anything, this was more frustrating, knowing that your work was still intact even as you were forced to abandon it and return to DOS. And for many of you, DOS was a place you had bought Windows to stay out of.

Win 3.1 embodies some major changes that make it truly (almost) robust. To begin with, it only runs in protected mode. That means you need a 286 or better machine. (If you want windowing on a lesser machine, buy GeoWorks.) That also means Windows has a chance of detecting misbehaving applications before they damage everything else. More importantly, it actually removes the applications to a more secure level of protection. Win 3.0 made little or no use of protection features available in advanced Intel processors, but simply took advantage of the memory management facilities to let you run multiple or large applications. That meant a fault in your word processor could actually put a bullet through the Windows code, leaving the computer catatonic. In Win 3.1 that can't happen. A normal application can no longer gain access to the areas of memory in which Windows itself executes—at least not without some antisocial behavior on the part of the programmers who wrote it. An application may still fail, but it won't take out other applications or Windows if it does. In this respect, life under Win 3.1 is no worse than DOS. In fact, you can now reboot individual applications under Windows. Press Ctrl-Alt-Del and you get the option of closing the thing you've been working on or restarting the whole machine.

You still may find that Windows doesn't want you to continue, and it may suggest closing all the applications and starting over. At least now you can close them in an orderly fashion, saving all your work as you go. To be truly robust even this sort of collateral nuisance must be eliminated. But with Win 3.1 the extermination of innocent data appears to have come to an end, and a safe multitasking and visually rich computing environment for IBM and compatible machines is at hand.

Details

The good news is that after seven years of fine-tuning, Win 3.1 anticipates most of the pitfalls of installation. But there are always new things out there that could not be foreseen or adequately dealt with before release. If you have a laptop with APM (advanced power management) features, Win 3.1 will recognize it, but you'll need to configure a few things. The same goes for certain memory managers, EMS software, SCSI drives, and CD-ROM drives.

One more thing about installation, concerning the Windows swapfile: Windows constantly tries to optimize itself, mostly according to its own logic, by swapping dormant bits and pieces of code and data to disk. This is called "virtual memory" and, specifically, it means creating a very large file. If you choose the quick installation, you may not be aware of this, but as much as 14 megabytes of disk space will be swallowed. The default status of this swapfile is "temporary," meaning if you exit Windows the file is erased. That may be what you want, but there is a penalty for leaving the file temporary—the file might be highly segmented, broken up into many small pieces, and this can seriously degrade performance. If you do a custom installation, you can make the file permanent, and it will usually be created in one large piece, which is what you want. (You can ensure this by running a defragger such as Norton Speed Disk, before you run the Windows setup.) You can also set the file to permanent later through Control Panel in the Main Group. Double-click on the 386 Enhanced icon, then on the Virtual Memory button. It's best if the swapfile is made permanent and as large as Windows recommends. If you hear a lot of disk activity when you are doing nothing, that is Windows accessing the swapfile. Buying more RAM will help minimize this time-consuming activity.

Program Manager

The novelist F. Scott Fitzgerald once wrote, "Life is best viewed through a single window." In Microsoft's opinion, that window is Program Manager, which is to Windows what COMMAND.COM is to DOS. What Windows is a window on has never been certified by Microsoft, and the failure to officially adopt a subordinate metaphor, such as "desktop," seems deliberate on its part. We might see anything. Which leaves us more or less as newborns, with precious little understanding of what we're looking at through our single window or how it all coheres.

Program Manager is "task oriented"—one does word processing, uses spreadsheets, telecommunicates, works on a database. To facilitate this simple view of what one does on one's computer, Program Manager arrives with things organized as groups of applications. To write something, one locates one's proper group—say, everything related to Microsoft Word—double-clicks on the program to execute it, then opens a file and begins writing.

You might think this was the only way to look at work on a personal computer, and it may feel oddly disjointed. For, of course, real life works quite differently. You start out to get some work done and then the interruptions begin—the phone, the boss, the kids. You adapt, and that's what a multitasking environment such as Windows was meant to address—the complex nature of real work and the need each of us feels to organize the way that works best for us.

You need to decide which philosophy suits you, and that's why there are alternatives to Program Manager—Norton Desktop, HP's New Wave, and others—all built around more refined concepts of the personal computing world in the window. But, for now, let's look at life on the computer from Microsoft's official point of view.

Each of the symbols, or icons, in Figure 1.1 represents a "group" of programs or files installed by SETUP.EXE, or by running Windows Setup in the Main group, or by the user selecting File from the Program Manager's pull-down menu, then New, then Program Group. No one (other than Microsoft) said this was going to be simple. What's in a group is as fluid as social dynamics in high school. You can drag and drop items from one group to another, or copy an item by holding down the Ctrl key as you drag—a program or file can be a member of more than one group. But, no groups within groups allowed—"nesting," in the jargon of operating systems and Tupperware. While this makes Progman (aka Program Manager) democratically thin and flat in terms of hierarchies, it also means you run out of shelf space fast.

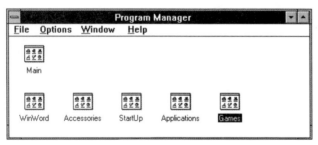

Figure 1.1   Windows Program Manager

The screen gets cluttered with groups—or the groups get stuffed with so many files and program icons that they are no longer "groups" in any meaningful sense, merely shelves full o' stuff.

THE MAIN GROUP

The Main group is where the principal set of utilities for controlling Windows are shelved (Figure 1.2).

 Read Me File

This is the manufacturer's warning label. Not a program, the Read Me file icon belongs to Windows Write, one of the default "associations" made by the initial Setup program. Double-click on it, and Windows will launch Write, a rudimentary word processor, with a document listing all the hardware and software compatibility problems known at the time of shipment of your Windows package. If you bought your computer with Windows installed, you'll probably be all right until you start adding things to the system yourself. If you're adding Windows to a mature system, it is essential that you check the Windows Read Me file immediately. You may have a conflict.

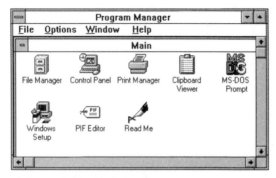

Figure 1.2   Main group

This list is not definitive, and in all fairness, it never could be. There are simply too many possible combinations of hardware and software. Microsoft can't check them all, and it is not in a position to cure many of the problems. Compatibility is a hard-won achievement, and that is why people who work with these machines day in and day out are cautious about changing hardware and software. You should be, too.

 ## File Manager

This is where you do most of the things you would do at the C:> prompt in DOS: view directory listings, copy, delete, rename files, make and remove directories, and format disks. DOS users instinctively seek this window, because it resembles programs such as XTree and Norton Commander, with all the familiar hierarchies. Prior to Win 3.1, File Manager was a poor substitute for those DOS shells and was one of the primary reasons people booted Windows off their disk.

Not any more. File Manager has been improved in two important ways: You can open multiple drive windows and you can move files by "dragging and dropping" like the Mac.

Select one or more files or directories with the mouse and then drag them by holding down the left mouse button until the little file icon covers some other directory or file or is over the window representing a separate drive or directory. When you release the mouse button, you will get a dialog box asking if you really want to copy. Click on the Yes button and the data will be duplicated. Hold down the Shift button while doing this and the file will be moved (a little plus in the file icon indicates a *copy* operation; its absence means a *move*). This is close to the way it should be. In any case, it's a vast improvement over previous versions. You can actually get work accomplished without the urge to resort to DOS. And for the uninitiated computer user it is, in some ways, more obvious what is taking place.

In the following example (Figure 1.3), I've copied a cardfile from the root of A: to C:\Windows.

A pair of warnings concerning File Manager: When you get confident, you can even turn off the "Are you sure...?" prompts. This is for people who don't keep their seat belts buckled when they fly or drive. If you're a hard knocks kind of person who can take lumps with your lessons, go ahead. All others, stick with the prompts and *think* before you click on Yes. I know the nattering is tiresome, but here's one place where the advantage of a graphical user interface (GUI) such as Windows over the command line interface (DOS) is doubtful. In fact, it

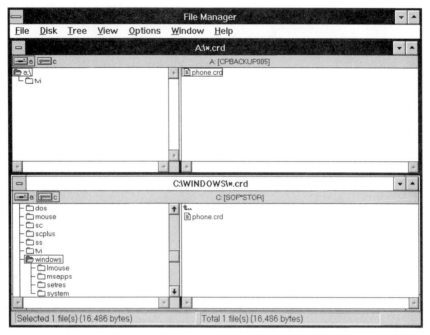

Figure 1.3 Open multiple windows in File Manager

illustrates the deep conflict some of us feel abandoning DOS. It is as if we were abandoning civilization itself.

❑ *Graphical User Interfaces: The Electronic Wall*

The Artificial Intelligence community is unevenly divided into two camps, the "NeuralNet/Perceptron" believers, and the "Rule-Based/Language" community. That's because civilized humans are, at root, dual in nature. Like all animals, we are pattern recognizers, possessed of a rich sensual life. Unique among animals, we are culturally rule-based, having classified our sensory data as wisdom, observation, and law, by sharing and refining the expression of individual experiences not merely over a lifetime, but across 150 million years, across continents, in gesture, symbol, and, finally, word, spoken and written. It has been a journey from frightful, uncomprehending, primordial darkness to enlightenment, a journey each of us is expected to repeat, with some degree of success, in roughly our first 22 years.

While an average college graduate is not exactly the culmination of all human experience, he or she is a lot closer to that ideal than the average Amazonian Indian, and it is written language that makes a semblance of this great human journey possible. If we had to experience it all—literally, sense all that had been sensed by all who came before us, anew—we could never progress. We would live as aboriginals in an insular present, hunting and gathering on the sharp edge of the mythical and magical world, as do children. And, while there are certainly lessons to be drawn from such innocents, this is not a state to which most of us would wish to be condemned.

That is precisely what falling into the embrace of a graphical user interface, such as Windows, represents—the abandonment of the written word, of meaningful phrases, of the most simple declarative sentence, in favor of signs and symbols that might have come off the wall of King Tut's tomb or from deep in some cave near Dordogne. Worse, the iconography of the computer GUI inherits little of any human past with which we are familiar. Though they tip their hat to every discipline from geometry to necromancy, the people who draw the little bit maps we click on are nothing more than commercial sign makers, and all their icons and buttons hieroglyphics on some virtual Tower of Babel. Don't get the idea they are inventing some new continuity of experience and expression, because if any of them copies or even alludes to the ideas contained in another's work, they'll be sued! Enter a GUI and you begin to endure life as commercial art.

While it's true a picture can be worth ten thousand words, there are damn few pictures that can do the work of ten words. Words have meaning. Words can be precise. Even in pseudolanguages such as DOS, commands are unambiguous. `Delete c:\express2\*.mci` means, exactly, delete all files with an `mci` extension in the `express2` directory on my `C:` drive. No worries about what pixel the tip of the mouse cursor is located over; no worries about whether, inattentively, I'm pointing at the `D:` drive window by mistake; no worries about whether I've highlighted the wrong thing and it has scrolled off the screen where I won't notice it. No worries because there's no ambiguity.

Equally true that, as you got used to using wildcards in DOS, life could get problematic; you might get carried away, type

`DELETE C:\WORD\*ED.DOC`, and blow away all your word processing files. But there was always an easier, safer way. And once you'd come to play fast and loose with wildcards, you still had to construct that command with some kind of precision, or it just plain wouldn't execute. It doesn't take any brains or thought at all to highlight a bunch of things and hit the Delete button. And most of us pay no more attention to the nattering in Windows than we did in DOS—a double-click means "Do it, damnit!" Do what? Make all those colored bits on my screen go away, of course. What, exactly, do those colored bits mean? Well, obviously, they mean what they mean...whatever that means. Click on one and find out.

The point, here, is the feeling I have of being thrust back into the cave. On the electronic wall before me is this rebus— images, bits of words, signs and symbols. Clearly, some intelligence has been at work, and if I want to get out of here alive I'm going to have to decipher their meaning. I don't think it's accidental that civilization went from cave painting to hieroglyphics to phonetic alphabets, and not the other way around. Now we have been sent back in the opposite direction. In the grips of the GUI we are all Indiana Jones, and our future and our livelihoods, if not our lives, depend upon understanding what some geek at Microsoft meant when they said [icons], before the blades whip out of the walls and take a slice of us.

Also, you can select what kinds of files you want to display, including hidden system files. You could, for instance, elect to show only document files or dBASE files. If you customize this way, remember there may be things on your disks that you are not seeing. It is easy to forget, especially on floppy drives. You think a disk is blank because no files show in the directory, and so you format it. Big mistake!

Below is a another good example of what's right with Windows and GUIs in general (Figure 1.4). Here I've asked the File Manager to show me all the files in the root directory of `C:`, sort them by size, and display their attributes. Notice the files marked with the exclamation point! These are hidden system files—two in particular, `IO.SYS` and `MSDOS.SYS`, are the principal DOS files used to boot your computer. Not only can you see them here, you can, if you want, change their attributes by selecting one with the mouse, choosing File in the pull-down menu and then Properties (File|Properties).

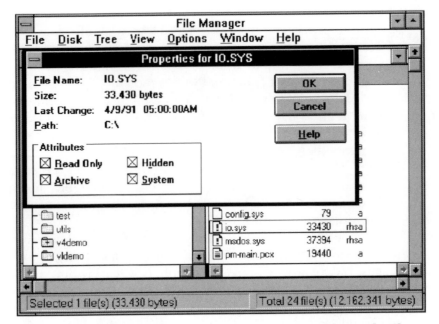

Figure 1.4 Viewing the properties of IO.SYS through File Manager

We not only have complete information about the file, including last modification date, but four check boxes showing which attributes are set. We can alter them, if we want, to make the files visible and even writeable. This is not so easy in DOS. And while it may rarely be necessary to deal with hidden system files, there are occasions when it is needed, and Windows makes it child's play.

File Association

Under the File|Associate menu, you can specify what file extensions belong to what programs by clicking on Associate (Figure 1.5).

Associating a file with an application has been a feature of Windows from the beginning, but it just wasn't clear how ordinary mortals could take advantage of anything beyond the canned associations made during installation. For example, .WRI files automatically belong to Windows Write. You can simply click on a file with that extension and Windows Write is launched to display it. You can actually do that for any program, but in versions of Windows prior to Windows 3.x, you had to modify the WIN.INI file. That's no longer the case.

In Figure 1.5, .DOC files are recognized as belonging to Word for Windows. In File Manager, the little icon that denotes the file will change from a blank, dog-eared page to one with lines, like this 📄 .

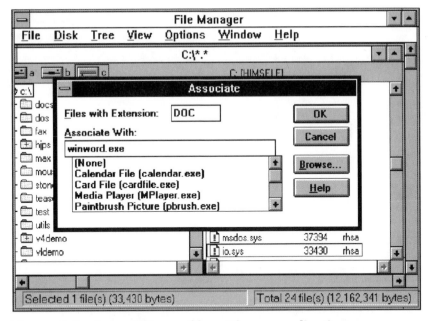

Figure 1.5   Associating a file with an application

This means the file is associated with a program. You don't have to look for the program, execute it, and load the file—simply double-click on the file or highlight the file and select File|Run, and that file's correct program will also be launched automatically.

The same is true of printing a file that's been associated with an application. Just select File|Print, and the program will be launched, the file opened, and the print dialog box presented.

The point here is that Windows breaks down some of the linearity you were accustomed to in DOS—a linearity born of typing. While it has its own tyrannies, there are more ways than one to do things in Windows, and it is this variety that makes Windows appealing.

Windows Help

Speaking of Windows' special tyrannies, if there's something you're not sure about, Help is just a mouse click away, sort of. What you get in Windows instead of linearity is hierarchies. Things are subordinated under other things, frequently *way* under, to prevent you from having to literally face them until and unless you want to. That is good and bad, and nothing more exemplifies this than *Help*.

It is good that Help is there on-line when you need it (Figure 1.6). And it is context-sensitive, meaning if you are doing something, say in the

Figure 1.6   Windows Help

File|Associate menu, clicking on the Help button shows you informa-
tion about that specific operation. The bad news is the information you
get is often written in computer bureaucratese. Worse, if you don't get the
help you want or need, break out a ball of twine and tie one end to something, because you are going on a mystical journey into the labyrinth of

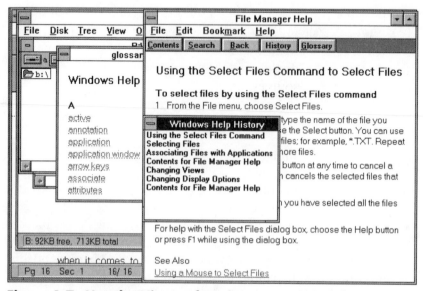

**Figure 1.7   Use the History function to navigate the maze
of Windows Help**

the Windows Help facility, and there is no knowing where—or when—you will re-emerge—or, alas, if you will ever find what you seek.

Actually, Help has a built-in ball of string, called History (Figure 1.7).

As you make your way down through the maze of categories and sub-categories, Windows adds the topic to the top of its history list. You can return to a previous selection by clicking on the History button, and when the dialog box appears, double-clicking on the topic where you think you went astray. It's also worth your while to mark commonly visited areas of Help by clicking on Bookmark. This leaves an entry under the Bookmark menu that will take you straight there in the future.

The main problem is that there's no way to get a view of the overall hierarchy of Help information. And that hierarchy itself is as arbitrary as Windows' design. What I'm saying is, until you've wandered Help's corridors and learned where things are located, you're going to feel (and be) a little lost. Just remember, you can use Help|History to re-trace the maze back to the point where you feel you went astray.

 Control Panel

This is the utility equipment room for Windows, the place where all the circuit breakers and thermostats are located, where the carpet sweeper and dustpan are stored, the weed killer along with the lawn sprinkler timer. If there's something you want to change about the way Windows looks and behaves (or makes your application look and behave), this is where you'd look first (Figure 1.8).

Windows keeps an internal list of system resources, and Windows applications are constantly referring to this list to determine how they should operate. Control Panel is where you add to, subtract from, and alter that list of resources.

 Color

This lets you customize the color of each separate element on your Windows screen: title bars, boxes, text, etc. You can choose from a dozen pre-designed color-coordinated schemes or concoct your own. There are some useful defaults here for those with LCD or plasma screens where "colors" are simulated—as they are here, in grayscale (Figure 1.9).

You can also customize the Windows color palette itself—but beware of side-effects with painting and scanning software. No matter how richly endowed your monitor or video card is with colors, you'll get only 20 from basic Windows, and messing with them can produce

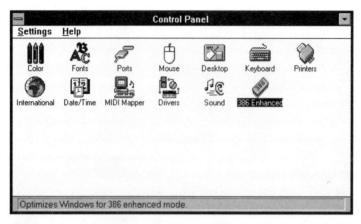

Figure 1.8   Control Panel contains utilities to change Windows' appearance and behavior

laughable results. Other "colors" are often faked with dithering—you will see them only when using applications that support additional colors from within Windows, but never in Progman or Fileman or anything else included in Windows.

 Fonts

This lets you determine which fonts are installed—that is, what your word processor or other applications list under Fonts. You can browse through what's available and see examples, along with how much disk

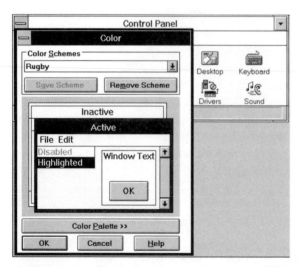

Figure 1.9   The Color menu in Control Panel

space the font files consume. You can remove fonts from the system, which frees system resources, meaning memory. You can add new fonts. And you can control whether True Type fonts are used at all, or used exclusively.

True Type is new with Windows 3.1—Microsoft's shot across the bow of Adobe, which had been the principal purveyor of scalable font packages, first in PostScript for printers, and then with the promise of Display PostScript. After much industry intrigue and falling in and out of bed with Apple, Microsoft has delivered true what-you-see-is-what-you-get fonts both on-screen and on paper, even with non-PostScript printers and at relatively cheap prices.

Be careful here. If your documents appear blank or no fonts are listed in your word processor, check to be certain you have fonts installed. And check to make sure you haven't selected True Type as the exclusive font. Some older applications might not handle True Type fonts.

 Ports

This is a simple one, this function, and an improvement over the DOS way of dealing with ports. You see icons representing communications and printer ports in the Ports panel, and boxes enclose the ones that are presently selected (Figure 1.10). You can even get advanced

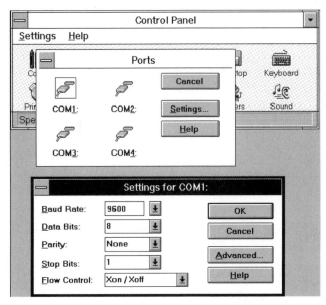

Figure 1.10 The Ports panel permits easy access to port settings

information about the processor port and IRQ level associated with each installed port and change that information if necessary.

This beats the DOS MODE command by a kilometer.

 International

For the balance of non–North American humanity, Microsoft allows some localization of Windows in the International panel (Figure 1.11).

Select a country from the Country list, and the date, time, and keyboard character formats are customized to that culture. Or set each individually, including standard paper size for the printer.

Note: A Japanese kanji-based version of Windows has just been released.

 Date/Time

This is simply where the system date and time are set.

 MIDI Mapper

MIDI stands for Musical Instrument Digital Interface. If you didn't know that already, you'll want to leave this icon alone for the present. If you did, this is where you'll come to set up MIDI devices, patch, and key maps.

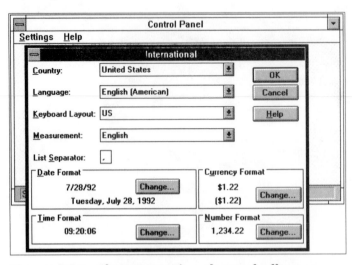

Figure 1.11 The International panel allows you to localize Windows to a particular culture.

Sound

If you have a sound card installed, such as AdLib, Sound Blaster, Covox, or the ATI F/X card, you can force Windows to play digitized sound samples whenever certain events occur, such as entry and exit from Windows itself, or when a keyboard error is made, or when certain error dialog boxes pop up bearing question marks or exclamations. If you find this little bit of cleverness irritating, you can stop it by turning off system sounds and associating the events with <none>.

 Drivers

This tool lets you add, remove, and set up software drivers for sound and video enhancement cards. Typically, if you install a sound board or specialized video enhancement card, you must install the associated driver here or the card won't work.

 386 Enhanced

If you don't already know it, Win 3.x was the first version of the program optimized for the Intel 80386 microprocessor. I have the impression that fewer and fewer people these days understand the significance of this information. Microprocessors, like the engines in our cars, are valued solely for their efficiency and brute horsepower. But the 386 has some special advantages. It is the first Intel processor designed from scratch since the advent of the IBM PC family of personal computers. Earlier chips were designed in hopes some customer might want to use them; the 386 was designed specifically to make a better PC. It was given not only memory protection features, but the ability to emulate multiple PCs, each running a program at the same time. You could say in some sense it was designed for Windows—there's no doubt Microsoft offered advice on the design. For you, all this is more or less invisible, except in this Control Panel item; this is where the hardware meets the hands, where you can actually adjust how Windows makes use of the 386's special design properties.

Time-Slicing

"Emulate" is the key word. Your computer only runs one application at a time. But it can switch from one to another literally in a millisecond, making it appear as if many things were happening simultaneously. This is called time-slicing, and you can set the thickness of the slices here. You can also determine the portions delivered to Windows and non-Windows applications when Windows is in the foreground and when it is in the background (Figure 1.12).

What you're doing here is setting priorities. You get to say when Windows is in the foreground and active, what share of available time goes to it, and what is left over for DOS applications. You can also say what share of time Windows should get when it is in the background. This can be important with communications and calculating applications. You want to make sure they get enough processor time to do useful work. You also don't want whatever you are working on to become sluggish in behavior because the background task is getting all the processor's attention. Note, however, that Windows depends on each running application to surrender control of the computer on a regular basis, so other applications might have a chance.

Predictably, many applications don't do this, making it difficult or impossible for other tasks to run. Other operating systems, such as OS/2, actually interrupt and transfer control, ready or not. This is the way it should be.

Device Contention

The 386 Enhanced section is also where you control device contention. Device contention is what happens when you have more than one application running, each trying to access a device (say, your printer) at the same time. Now, even with a multitasking operating environment,

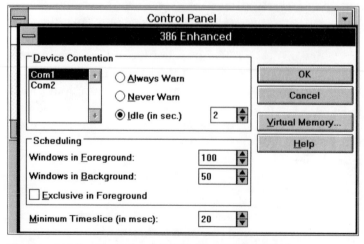

Figure 1.12 Use the 386 Enhanced panel to control Window's time-slicing

you can't print two documents on the same printer at the same time. Here's where you can set Windows to notify you if such a contention for resources is occurring.

Virtual Memory

The Virtual Memory button lets you control the amount of Virtual (disk) Memory available in 386 Enhanced mode (Figure 1.13).

For those of you who don't already know it, Virtual Memory is really a file on the hard disk. When Windows needs RAM space to run an application, it takes a piece of some program out of RAM and sticks it on the disk in a swapfile. Windows tries to be intelligent and only swaps things that haven't been used lately or that are marked by the programmers as being swappable. This means you can have many utilities, files, and applications open on the desktop, even when their total memory requirements vastly exceed the amount of RAM in your computer. Like a fish beneath the surface of a pond, this memory is virtual because, while it is there, it is not where you perceive it to be.

This isn't as arcane as it looks or sounds. Memory is memory; it holds bits and bytes. The RAM "memory" chips in your computer are fast and volatile, while your disk is slow, and more or less permanent. But they both hold the same stuff. Normally we load from disk to RAM and save from RAM to disk. While it may seem new to you, computers have been faking RAM with disk files for decades, since the days when RAM chips (what was once known as core memory) were prohibitively expensive.

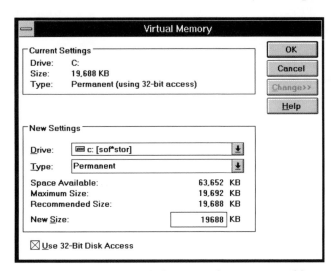

Figure 1.13 Control the Windows swapfile with the Virtual Memory panel

Typically, this is done with clever software, and Windows is nothing if not clever. So creating a swapfile is like adding very slow RAM chips to your computer. You can get more and larger programs and data to run. What Windows does is keep track of which portions of fast RAM are being used and which are not. When it needs more memory, it swaps a chunk of fast RAM to the swapfile and loads what was requested into the vacated RAM space. Now, this can and does get time consuming—"churning the disk," in computer jargon. You can hear it. This is also what is happening when you hear your hard disk do something when you are not touching the computer. You can improve the efficiency of the process by doing two things:

- Make the swapfile as large as Windows recommends.
- Make the swapfile permanent.

The larger the swapfile, the more efficiently Windows runs. And when it's permanent, the swapfile will be created in a single contiguous piece. "Temporary" swapfiles can be "fragmented"; in computer parlance, this means that they occupy two or more pieces of disk space in different physical locations. Since the slowest thing your computer does is move the read/write disk heads from one place to another picking up pieces of data, a lot of this sort of thing can slow Windows to a crawl.

Now, a permanent swapfile can only be as large as the biggest chunk of contiguous disk space. So, if you are installing Windows onto a "mature" system where the hard disk is almost full, you are going to have to delete some things to make room, and you most likely will have to run a defragger (a program that reorganizes the physical location of files and pieces of files on your hard disk). Most commercial defraggers don't like Windows (NoFrag, which is included with this book, is an exception). With others you have to exit Windows. Don't just double-click on the MS-DOS icon—that won't work.

As I said, earlier, that's a pain. One of the reasons we work in Windows is to avoid DOS. And that is why I wrote NoFrag. Not only does it run within Windows, it runs in the background, meaning you can do other things while it works. It is actually safer than commercial DOS defraggers, and it will pack all the open space into a single block where your permanent swapfile can live and grow happily.

32-Bit Access

When running MS-DOS under Windows, the 32-Bit Disk Access box lets you run and switch between applications faster by optimizing disk performance. Some hard disk controllers don't support this feature and Windows will omit showing this option if it detects a non-supportive disk controller.

 ## Print Manager

You may not realize it at first, but Print Manager is one of the key features of Windows. No matter what application you run, when it comes time to print, Print Manager is called on to do the job—unless you disable it. This is not like DOS, where each application is programmed to handle the printer itself. In fact, Print Manager illustrates how different the Windows environment really is. Programs under Windows do not control or "own" the hardware; Windows is the sole proprietor, not only of the printer (or printers), but of the screen, the keyboard, mice, graphic tablets, scanners, and whatever other wonders we can dream up. These are all "resources" that Windows must allocate. Of course, the principal resource is time, both yours and the processor's, and what Print Manager does is borrow some from whatever you are doing to talk to the resources—in this case, your printer.

Figure 1.14 shows a typical Print Manager screen, with several documents queued for printing in the order they were received. Print Manager will take little bits of time from whatever you are doing to send the documents to the printer. If you have a fast computer and a printer with a large memory buffer, it will appear, magically, that there is no penalty for printing while you work on something else.

Unlike what you've been accustomed to in DOS programs, Windows does not ordinarily use the built-in printer fonts, but prints everything

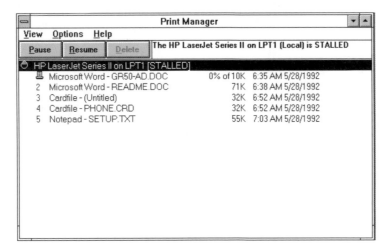

Figure 1.14   A Print Manager queue

as a bit-mapped image—that is, a dot at a time, even if it is only text. This is inherently ten times as arduous as sending a stream of text to be printed with the printer's own default font. Check the Print Manager|Options setting. You can assign a low, medium, or high priority to print jobs (the default is "high"). Low means only printing when nothing else is happening, medium splits time 50/50, and high effectively stops everything until the printing is done. You still have the option of pausing and switching to a different task if, for some reason, you change your mind and want to do something else immediately

If you have an older, slower machine, it might be best to disable printing in the background. You can do this in Win 3.1 with Control Panel|Printers by deselecting Use Print Manager. This causes each document to be printed the minute you command, and all other activities to be suspended until the printing is done.

 ## Clipboard Viewer

The Clipboard is simply a scratch pad that Windows provides as a resource to all Windows applications. Whenever you cut and paste or copy something somewhere in Windows, the material you move is saved to the Clipboard and can be viewed there. The information can be text, rich text with formatting information, or a bit-mapped image and its color palette. The contents of the clipboard can be given a name and saved permanently. The Clipboard's greatest drawback is that only one clipping remains on the board; as soon as you cut or copy a second image, the first is erased.

Note: A keyboard shortcut exists for copying the image of the active window. ALT-Print Screen will copy it to the Clipboard and Print Screen will paste it in somewhere else.

 ## The DOS Prompt

Depending on your background, this is either your blessed escape hatch to the familiar universe of DOS or the trap door that drops you into DOS's inky and dangerous waters. Type EXIT and press Enter and you are back in Windows.

You actually never left. When you click on the MS-DOS prompt, Windows tries to create a hermetic DOS world that looks and feels to all applications like the real thing. A neat trick here is to make the DOS world run in a window under Windows. You do that by using the Alt-Tab key combination, instead of EXIT, to switch back to Windows from the

DOS screen. This reduces DOS to an icon. Now click once on the icon and choose Settings.

Here you can choose to put DOS in a window to let it run tasks in the background while you do something else, allocate time, and if all else fails, terminate the DOS Window with extreme prejudice (Figure 1.15).

Before DOS terminates you? As I was writing this I switched back and forth to a windowed DOS prompt several times and was rewarded with the dreaded STOP sign, indicating I had crashed the computer so thoroughly that only turning it off would cure it. Consequently, I've had the pleasure of writing this section twice. The spice of life is Windows, some days.

Most applications that do not use some protected mode memory feature will run in the DOS window. In fact, you can put most of them into a resizable window, although I've seen strange things when you try to use a mouse. And then are a few things you simply cannot or should not attempt: running CHKDSK with the /f option, running programs that alter the disk, such as defraggers and disk editors, and deleting temporary files.

 Windows Setup

If you change anything once you've installed Windows, video or mouse hardware, countries, networks, or simply your mind, this is where you come to straighten it all out. If it's a video card you want to change, be sure to come here before you do it; otherwise you may not be able to see what you're doing and you'll have to reinstall Windows all over again—not the pain it once was, but still no great pleasure.

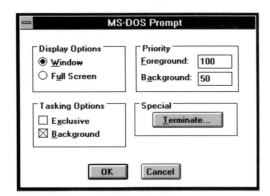

Figure 1.15 Control the DOS window on the MS-DOS Prompt panel

Video card and network installation options are based on a set of standard drivers supplied with Windows and optional drivers supplied by the card manufacturers. If you don't see the options offered, then you haven't got the drivers installed.

PIF Editor

All non-Windows applications require a Program Information File, a .PIF. This is a description, for Windows' benefit, of how to deal with the fact that the application probably knows nothing about graphics and is almost certainly ignorant of what Windows is up to managing memory, COM and Printer ports, and other system resources.

When IBM and Microsoft invented the .PIF, it was all anyone talked about. Now you hardly hear a word, but it is one of the most powerful and useful features of Windows for people trying to integrate their older DOS applications into a Windows environment. DOS applications need a .PIF to run under Windows. If the application does not come with a .PIF, Windows uses a default set of standards. You can create a .PIF file yourself with the PIF Editor, or modify an existing one. Either way, you'll want to make extensive use of Windows' HELP facilities to get a grip on what each parameter actually controls.

STARTUP GROUP

This is such a no-brainer that one wonders that it took until Windows 3.1 to implement. You can drag and drop any application into the window and it will automatically start every time you launch Windows. If you want it to start with a particular file, open then drag that file into the StartUp group; as long as the file extension is associated with a program it will launch itself. While Windows comes with a potfull of associations already made, you can create them yourself by adding the program and its peculiar extension to the WIN.INI file under [Extensions] with SYSEDIT or any text editor.

ACCESSORIES GROUP

Americans are surpassed only by the Japanese in the apparent belief that happiness and success are directly related to the number of gizmos and gadgets they possess. Windows is a gadget lover's paradise. The Accessories Group is chock-full of gizmos and utilities (Figure 1.16).

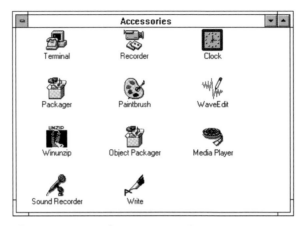

Figure 1.16   The Accessories group

 Calendar

This gizmo is nothing more than a daily to-do sheet or a display of the month's days and dates. While simplicity is a virtue, this accessory proves too much of any virtue can be a vice. It doesn't offer much more in the way of jotting space than your desktop calendar—except that you don't throw it out each year.

 Notepad

For those of you who prefer Windows Write to a full-scale word processor, look at Notepad, the next step down. It does very little, and it does it well. Don't worry about fonts and formatting (you have no access to them), but also don't worry about getting lost in some software designer's purgatory of an interface; this tool is simple, simple, simple.

 Cardfile

A rudimentary index card program, not customizable at all. The nicest thing you can say about it is that it works as a good rudimentary phone and address book—which is perhaps the best kind.

 Calculator

The simplest of calculators. It's functional for basic math operations, but not well programmed to take advantage of the 10-key keypad that comes with most keyboards this decade. There seems to be no way to CLEAR or CLEAR ENTRY except by changing from 10-key to mouse, which greatly degrades speed of operation, especially for an experienced 10-key user.

 ## Terminal

I have wasted more time and energy trying to telecommunicate via modem than in any other single task on a PC. Windows Terminal is not the solution to that nightmare. If you're wondering what telecommunications via modem is all about or happen to get stuck on the road without a real communications program, this will work. Otherwise, don't waste time and effort here; try ProComm Plus for Windows. 'Nuf said.

 ## Recorder

The idea behind Windows' Recorder is simple: Make a record of every keystroke and mouse movement, give it a filename, and allow it to be played back. DOS has had macro-recorder programs like this for years. The problem here is that the world of DOS is much simpler. Only one program can be running at a time, and rarely did the screen show more than one picture of what was happening, and it was text-based, not graphical. No worries about what the mouse was pointing at or where the keyboard input was being displayed. In Windows, who or what has the "input focus" among the many items on the screen can get quite complex. Add to that the likelihood that you've resized or moved some windows since you recorded your key- and mouse-stroke sequence and you begin to see the root problem.

Recorder is dumb. It presumes the mouse is in the same window and the original application is active at the same point as when you recorded. It also does not expect to get interrupted by pop-up activity from other applications—or you! In short, I found it nearly useless, though someone who does not multitask might make some use of it for replacing short, repetitive tasks.

 ## Clock

Tells time, for all you chronophiles.

Packager

Aka Object Packager, this lets you insert files, pictures, and icons in documents that support the Windows OLE (Object Linking and Embedding) standard. Like many of the accessories, this is a crude program developed during the early stages of OLE to give programmers something to make OLE real. Fortunately, any application that supports OLE already incorporates something like Packager, so you should never have to use this enigmatic, stand-alone version.

 Paintbrush

Like Terminal, this is not a serious or terribly useful program, but a teaser that dates back to the original release of Windows.

 Sound Editor

One of the first multimedia abilities Windows gained was sound, with the standard file having a .WAV extension. This is a basic .WAV file editor, and it falls in the category of being too advanced for people who know nothing about sound editing, and not advanced enough for those who do.

 Sound Recorder

This let's you make rudimentary .WAV file recordings, if you have a proper soundboard, such as Sound Blaster, Ad Lib, or Pro Audio Spectrum. Of course, those boards all have much better software bundled with them, so you wouldn't have to mess with this.

 Multimedia Control Panel

This is another of what I call "technology demonstrator" programs. It lets you play multimedia sound, MIDI, and other recordings with a VCR or CD-like control panel. But it's just a toy meant to suggest Windows' potential. In fact, that's the most irritating thing about the whole Accessory Group—it's a quintessential Microsoft tease. There's a suggestion of all this neat power latent in the product, none of it really usable today. Serious Windows communications programs have just hit the market in the last year, and they still underperform their DOS equivalents. Serious multimedia capabilities under Windows are a ways off; Windows is still too big, fat, and slow. Perhaps a 150-MHz Pentium machine will prove peppy enough to bring high-resolution color talkies to the Windows desktop, but that will be a while coming. If you buy for the promises, practice holding your breath. Multimedia for under $2000? Get a submarine—it's gonna be a few years.

Summary

These are the major functions and utilities that are part of Windows 3.1. Numerous other software products are available that replace, enhance, or add something totally different to Microsoft's basic package. The next section takes a look at various software that can be used to replace the functionality of the cornerstone of Windows: the Program Manager.

SECTION 2

Program Manager Alternatives

2

Norton Desktop

Overview

Charm School for Windows, Norton Desktop for Windows from Symantec, combines the features of Program Manager and File Manager and polishes Windows' interface etiquette. An improved drag and drop model and additional desktop utilities make executing choices easier and work faster than Windows 3.1 alone. Jeff found it charming; he also has a weakness for redheads. I thought it provided some useful incremental improvements under a lot of well-applied makeup. We agree, however, it has maddening flaws that stem from its DOS roots and fear of Apple's attorneys.

Details

It's the writer's job to do the Christian thing—suffer, so that others will not have to. True to that calling, Jeff and I made opposite choices during installation. I wouldn't let Program Manager be replaced; Jeff, a man wanting to experience the product in its fullest self-defined flowering, said okay. The results appeared dramatically different—Jeff's machine showed a bunch of folders and tool buttons, mine a bunch of group icons—so I tried installing Norton both ways myself. My machine came up looking the same as before, except when I said "no" to replacing Program Manager, I had to invoke Norton Desktop once Windows was running. When I said "yes" to replacement, I got help the first time Windows ran. Norton Desktop preserves existing Windows groups, so you hardly notice the disappearance of Progman, other than the handful of new icons to decipher (Figure 2.1).

How come Jeff's machine and mine appeared so different after installation and a few days use (Figure 2.2)?

The answer, of course, was that Jeff is also a Macintosh user, and he compulsively took advantage of Norton Desktop's extensions of the Mac drag and drop philosophy. The Mac (Norton Desktop) approach is discrete—one writes a letter, balances the checkbook, makes a phone call.... To accomplish these tasks, you find the file you want to write, drag-and-drop it on the desktop, and open it for writing, leaving it up to Windows to figure out what program belongs to what kind of file. As a result, an ordinary desktop looks something like Jeff's, or, once I'd got the idea and revised mine, like Figure 2.3.

Here's another philosophical peculiarity—what I think of as the vending machine metaphor in operation. You can execute things in Norton Desktop by dragging files and punching the right button on what Norton calls a "tool"—those icons on the right-hand side. Drag a file to the Viewer tool, for example, and the viewer window pops up

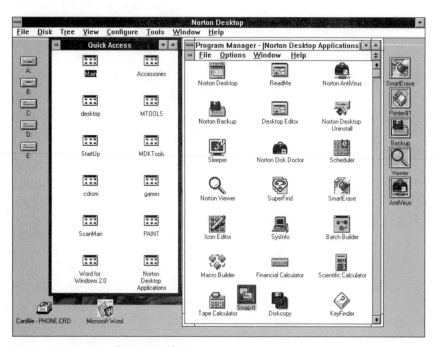

Figure 2.1   Paul's installation

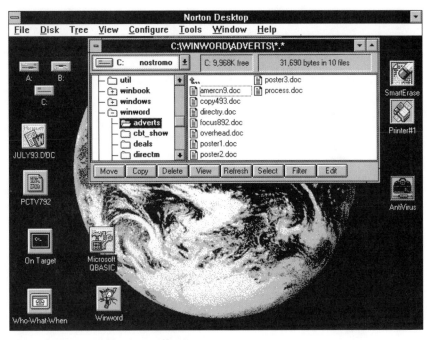

Figure 2.2 Jeff's installation

with the file displayed. Likewise, drag a .DOC to the Word for Windows tool, drop it, and Word runs the file.

So, the idea is, you array your desktop with your favorite tools, use the Drive and Viewer tools to locate files, then drag and drop to marry the two and, voila! they run.

To accomplish this, Norton Desktop for Windows anneals Progman and File Manager into a single dashboard instrument. Drives appear as icons. Double-click on them, and you get a typical tree directory.

Note the row of buttons across the bottom that let you perform most standard file-handling functions (Figure 2.4). You can customize which buttons appear at the bottom of this window. One default button of particular note is the View button. Click it, and you add a window that displays the file you're pointing at (Figure 2.5). In this case, it's a picture of the MS-DOS prompt.

Text files from a number of different document formats are recognized and displayed in recognizable form, as are database and spreadsheet files.

There are mouse drag-and-drop and keyboard shortcuts for many button functions; you also can select from the main pull-down menus or customize the button row to suit your preferences. This follows the philosophy that providing many ways to achieve the same result does

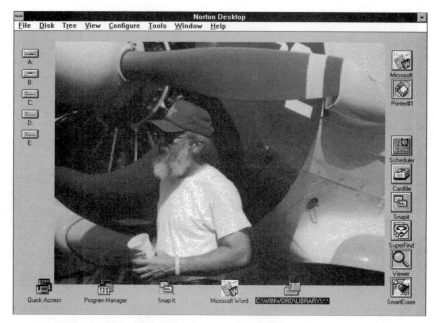

Figure 2.3   Drag and drop approach

not make a program more complex, but satisfies a wider variety of people or an individual's appetite for diversity.

Tools are also available from a tools menu, but you can customize which tools you want to appear as icons on your desktop. That customization is this product's greatest strength for individual users, and it poses its greatest drawback for large corporate sites that insist on standard configurations. The product is *so* customizable in every respect that looking at someone else's chosen configuration of NDW is confusing

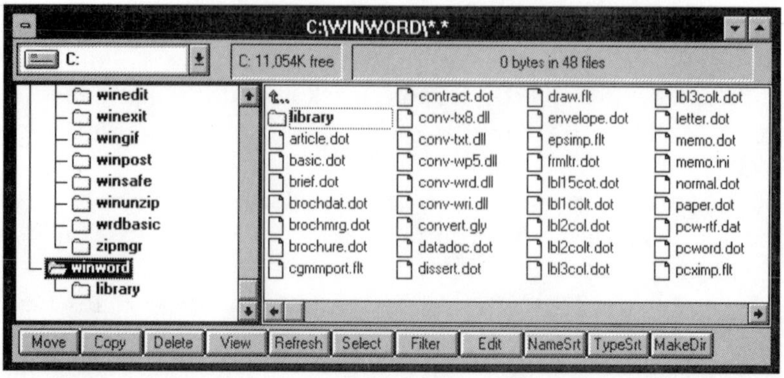

Figure 2.4   The marriage of Progman and File Manager

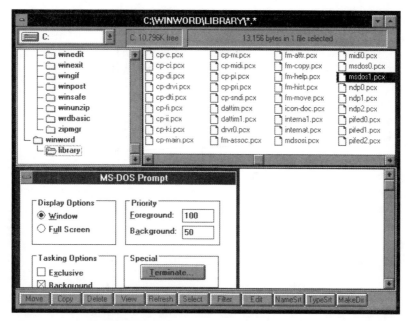

Figure 2.5 Using the View button

enough to make you think you've fallen through the looking glass, which is what Jeff and I experienced looking at each other's screens. We were both befuddled.

Some customizing options make for extremely productive use of Windows. Among these are the ability to add a menu item to launch an application from within another application. For example, if you frequently switch between a project management program like On Target and a word processor, you could have NDW's Launch Manager put them in your Control menu, the long dash button in the top-left corner of any application's window.

If you install both On Target and your word processor there, you can switch directly from one to the other. Windows, of course, lets you do this by pressing a sequence of Alt-Tabs, which rotate through all open activities. But if you tend to keep a lot of applications running at once, you might have to jump through a large number of these before you find the one you want. NDW's Launch List puts up a menu you can use either the mouse or customized keystrokes to select, or you can revert to Windows' Task Manager.

While the task of locating the file or data you want to work on is greatly simplified over Windows and dramatically easier than the same task in DOS, you will eventually encounter one of the shortcomings of Norton Desktop for Windows. It has limited power to associate files with programs. .DOC means Microsoft Word for Windows. You can change it to something else, but that extension can only have one meaning at a time.

Windows has a fair number of automatic associations: .DOC, as I said, means Word for Windows, .WRI means Windows Write, .PCX means Paintbrush, etc. You can change the associations or make new ones using the File|Associate option (Figure 2.6).

On the Mac, each document can be associated with a particular executable, and once that happens, the association sticks forever; so having multiple release versions of Lotus or Word on your machine at once poses little problem. Under Windows—even with Norton Desktop—you're stuck with either changing the associations every time confusion arises (either because multiple applications' data files use the same extension or were created in multiple versions of the application), or dragging multiple versions of a program onto your desktop.

The NDW screen (Figure 2.1) has a set of icons running down the right side for the utilities the vendor presumes you'll use often: Norton AntiVirus, SmartErase (an intelligent file erase utility that works as a holding area for files you ask to be erased), Viewer (a file viewer), Printer (a printer icon to which you can drag files and send them to the printer), Shredder (a secure file erase utility), and a copy of Norton Backup. On the upper-left part of your screen you'll find icons for your disk drives (graphically showing whether they're hard drives or 3.5- or 5.25-inch drives). Double-clicking on a drive icon opens up the NDW drive window for that device.

OTHER UTILITIES

No Norton utility would be complete without an overflowing kitchen sink-full of handy Norton stuff, such as AntiVirus, Backup, Desktop

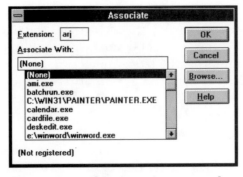

Figure 2.6 The associate panel

Editor, Norton Desktop Uninstall, Sleeper, Norton Disk Doctor, Scheduler, Norton Viewer, SuperFind, and others.

 ## Norton AntiVirus

This is a Windows version of Symantec's commercial anti-virus program. Install will invoke it as a default and place the tool on your desktop. If it says you have an infection, believe it and let the program "cure" your disk. No one should consider themselves immune to the problems associated with computer viruses, which range from pesky to lethal to your machine. Note, however, that in the course of a year new strains of maliciousness will have been created that this version of AntiVirus won't detect. You'll need to decide how valuable your work is and whether or not to upgrade.

A current and complete disk or tape backup of all your files is the only absolute insurance against a virus.

 ## Norton Backup

This is the Windows version of Symantec's Backup, thrown in as a bonus. It's vastly better than the backup program included with DOS 5.0 or earlier versions—so much better that Microsoft began bundling a version of Norton's with DOS 6.0.

 ## Desktop Editor

A rudimentary Windows text editor, it contains a useful text locating feature that will locate all files containing a certain key word or pattern.

 ## Norton Desktop Uninstall

For the unconverted, the ultimate power; it cleans Norton Desktop off your system. No serious software package should be sold without an uninstaller.

 ## Sleeper

Yet another Windows screen blanker. Don't use the password protection if you've got Windows' own blanker set to password protect, or no amount of abracadabra will get you into the system.

Norton Disk Doctor

This is a Windows version of Norton's automatic disk repair utility. Comes on a separate floppy, so you can make a stab at resurrecting unbootable machines. Programs like Disk Doctor are powerful and can be effective when disaster strikes. But you'll want to read the documentation before administering this medicine to any machine—and know that the cure, now and then, is worse than the disease.

 Scheduler

Scheduler will either perform regularly scheduled tasks automatically (say, back up your network hard drive at 1 A.M. Saturday night) or allow you to set it up to launch a reminder window at you so you don't forget that inexpensive, nineties trademark, the low-power lunch.

 Norton Viewer

This lets you look at text files and major spreadsheet and dBASE data files in native mode without having to get the creator program up and running. Viewer is placed on your desktop at installation time as a default tool.

 SuperFind

There's more than a little hyperbole here: This is a just simple file locator utility. *Useful,* not super.

 SmartErase

If you use this tool instead of DOS DELETE, the selected file will disappear from your directory listings but not from the disk. Norton moves it to a secret spot, to be purged on schedule—say every fifth day. This can save you from disastrous errors, such as deleting a critical file unintentionally, but it won't gain you any disk space, which is usually the reason you attacked your file system in the first place. Still, getting into this "soft delete" habit is a good thing. Ultimately some future refinement of this will become the standard.

Icon Editor

This is a mini pixel editor for creating or monkeying around with icons. Jeff is sure it's valuable for something, but can't figure out what, so considers Icon Editor basically digital onanism.

 SysInfo

This is a sweetly graphical version of the venerable Norton program that displays all you never wanted to know about your system, but technical support insisted upon having before they'd talk to you.

 Batch Builder

The product comes with a shell program called Batch Builder. Hundreds of thousands of corporate support people made their names building custom shells for DOS that insulated "dumb users" from the terrifying C: prompt. Given the complaint I have about Windows—that it's like a game of *Concentration* where you have to remember where everything is hidden—one could argue a support shell would be a useful thing.

On the other hand, Windows itself is being sold as a solution to a problem that required a shell. Batch Builder is powerful and cranky, and it can be very useful for programmers building custom interfaces for computer novices. It's not something you should dabble in unless you have a need.

 Macro Builder

Norton is also pushing the Macro Builder utility that's included in the package as an "easy way for even a novice user to automate and run common tasks." *I think not.* As a speedier way for programmers to build Batch Builder utilities, it's fantastic (as long as it doesn't require the user to exit to DOS). But if your user can't think like a programmer (the old sequence, selection, iteration model), he or she is going to be stuck in a corner in the fetal position, whimpering for support.

Calculators

Norton outscores Windows three-calculators-to-two. Your bonus is a financial calculator. Don't, however, throw away the old 10-key yet. One thing these three calculators have in common—you have to keep taking your right (wrong) hand off the keyboard to use a mouse. Even the ambidextrous will find the keyboard interface makes minimal sense.

 ## Diskcopy

Diskcopy is what it says, the old DOS standby—only inside Windows so you don't have to face the dreaded C: prompt. It makes identical copies of the contents of a floppy.

 ## KeyFinder

The Norton version of Windows' native Character Map, the Key Finder lets you get at all the odd funny little widgets such as © and ®, or ¥ if you have the yen.

 ## Format Disk

Again, a Windows equivalent for the DOS command for formatting diskettes.

 ## Shredder

A file security utility, this not only deletes all the data associated with the file, it erases the area of the disk the file occupied so it cannot be reconstructed by anyone short of the National Security Agency (which can extract data that has been overwritten up to six times).

 ## Backup Assistant

A scheduler for backup.

Full Backup

A shortcut for the backup program that simply launches it into a full backup of everything on every disk.

Finally, a word about NDW's on-line Help. Jeff found it almost useless, a small but tragic flaw because the package is so complex, including many features that are in locations you won't likely memorize. Instead of using the traditional, Windows hierarchical text-based help, Symantec got innovatively graphical, with all kinds of hieroglyphics to point and click on, which could have been a benefit if it had been well-executed, but it wasn't. I've heard rumors that many of these high-function, low-price Windows programs intentionally use underperforming on-line help as a copy-protection scheme, forcing a user to own the paper documentation.

Summary

Norton Desktop for Windows includes a convenience feature you'll probably never need: You can run an uninstall command and get rid of it entirely. While the program has far too many features to be a coherent whole (it's got that horrible feature-elephantiasis that contemporary utilities packages suffer from), it adds some good layers to the Windows interface, fixing some mutant Windows features that were probably put in there intentionally to avoid look-and-feel lawsuits. A stand-alone user with the desire to customize his or her desktop can have a lot of fun with this, and corporate support folk can build a shell around Windows to protect novice users.

3

Rooms for Windows

Overview

Rooms for Windows from XSoft provides a new way of looking at the way you work with Windows. You collect your programs and/or data files into groups called Rooms, in each of which you include all of the items you need for a logical set of functions—for example, accounting, business correspondence, proposal-writing and estimation, or programming. If you accept it as a simple product with a simple concept, it's a beautiful way to interact with Windows. If, however, you take the house/rooms metaphor too seriously, you'll be whipsawed by some counter-intuitive ways of doing things.

Details

My first reaction is, *Now here's something different!* You have to be careful, of course; much of what Windows is about is visual perception. Things can look wildly different but still behave in a most orthodox and maddeningly Microsoft fashion, conforming to the Redmond spin on the dictates of the "electronic desktop" thought up 20 years ago at Xerox's Palo Alto Research Center.

Rooms is the newest metaphor from Xerox PARC: the electronic floorplan. This is the desktop as embodied in the Ward and June Cleaver home.

You gather things, each unto a room of its own—programs, files, utilities. Need more room? Add one! They're all visible and accessible from the "Overview" room, which acts as a sort of lobby. "Overview" opens onto all rooms and all rooms have a door to the "Overview." You can cause a little door icon to appear in any room, leading to any other room. There's also a default room called "Overlay," and anything you place in it will be put automatically into all other rooms as icons. That's what the product does—a simple recasting of the Program Manager point of view, uncluttered by other, Tellerist (if a feature can be conceived and coded, it *must* be included) activity.

You can gather a collection of rooms into a "Suite" to be saved and loaded; but you only see one suite at a time. This being Xerox, I think the model the developers had in mind was an office tower, but there is nothing inherently hierarchical about Rooms, other than the fact that everything attaches to the "Overview" lobby. You are never more than two doors and four mouse clicks away from your destination.

It's an interesting concept. After all, most of us more or less arrange our lives this way—bedroom, bathroom, dining room, game room, family room, library. That's not how we necessarily *live* our lives, but I think we all accept the conventional wisdom that this messy overlap of form and function—eating in the kitchen, reading in the bathroom—is the result of having run out of room or of poor design. Rooms will let you test that belief.

Setup creates a Windows Rooms group within Program Manager, but when you click on the little door icon you enter a noticeably different realm. Welcome to the animistic universe of "Object-Orientation," where programmers turn our screens into primitive worlds where things appear to have a life of their own. If you just go mousing around and clicking on things, as I always do initially to see what they do, get ready for surprises—and, potentially, a mess that leads you to reinstall or throw Rooms on the shelf, or worse, defenestrate it entirely.

The default installation, shown in Figure 3.1, is two "Rooms" ordered alphabetically, "Overlay" then "Room 1" in the "Overview" room. No dragging and dropping here to order rooms—you're stuck with the alphabetic sequence. That means if you want things to appear in a certain order, you have to think of clever names (or use numbers as leading characters in room names) to get them floor-planned to suit.

I plunged ahead, as usual without reading the manual, and failed. Pointing and clicking on objects appeared to select them but did not make them active. Further clicking returned me to the starting place. Reading the ROOMINFO.WRI file explained that you can only activate an application by entering the room through a door or clicking on the

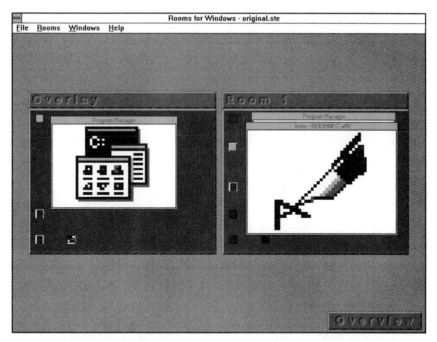

Figure 3.1 Default installation of Rooms for Windows

title bar in `Overview`. What I was doing was "expanding" a view of the rooms and icons, which lets you see what they are, but that's all. Any further keyboard or mouse activity "shrinks" what you're looking at.

It all makes sense after a fashion, but Rooms is unique enough in the way it behaves that it is better to read the first few chapters of the documentation and skip the frustration. The manual is simple, lucid, and well-organized, which, of course, is supported by the uncluttered, straight-ahead goals of the program.

The purpose of expanding and contracting is that unless you're gifted with x-ray vision, the tiny icons visible in each overview room are mostly indecipherable. That can be a plus. One problem with Windows is that it shows you more than you need to know at any one time—infoglut—or else covers everything up—*Concentration.* Rooms miniaturize. You can peek, you can move things from room to room by dragging and dropping, and you can copy things from one room to another.

This is where it gets confusing. While running Rooms, you look at something in Program Manager in one room, then switch to another room and there it is again. It follows you around because it is overlaid. There is only one copy of Progman running and any change in one place changes it in every room. If you remove it from one room, you may, depending on how you execute it, delete it from *all* rooms, for the same reason. It's disorienting to go from one room to the next and see the furniture, so to speak, spontaneously moved or missing. Especially when you are the only one in the house!

You can get around this particular challenge by executing a program from inside a room as its own separate instance, that has nothing to do with what's going on in other rooms. This is the conservative thing to do, but it uses the most system resources. You now have two versions of the same program running—Windows memory constraints permitting. While the two programs look alike at the moment they're copied, changes in one room will not affect the program in other rooms—unless, that is, you're working on a common file, then *watch out*. What happens next depends on how smart the program is. And you will probably be prompted to load SHARE.EXE from the DOS prompt.

The only way to tell the difference between overlaid, copied, and original instances of a program are subtle background color differences. Not good, not good at all!

In Room 1, XSoft conveniently loaded a Windows Write document, release notes for this version of Rooms for Windows (Figure 3.2). They also have a copy of Progman running. These behave in ordinary Windows fashion. But notice the other icons. We have a clock in the upper-

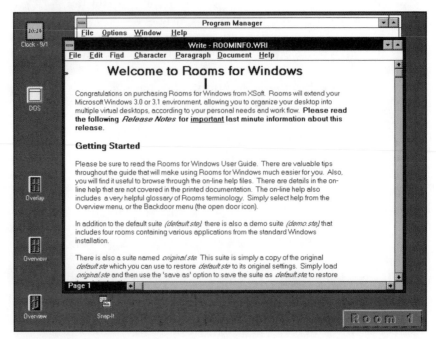

Figure 3.2   Room 1

left corner—this is actually located in Overlay, and, consequently, it will be included in every room to satisfy the chronophiles. There's a DOS button that does the expected, dumps you out to DOS.

There are also two door icons and these are important. One of them, labeled Overview, is the door to the lobby. This icon was created in the Overlay, so you automatically see it in every room. The other door, in the lower-left corner, is called the "back door." It always leads back to the room you came from, which in this case is also Overview. As a programmer, I found the concept of the back door logical, since I usually program in a back door to escape lock-up situations during development. Jeff, trying to take the metaphor more literally than the way it was presented, found the concept that the back door always leads backwards unreal. In real life, for Jeff anyway, the back door can lead back from where you came, but only if you entered a room *through* the back door.

That's basically it. You can also change rooms through a menu system attached to the title bars and icons, Windows fashion, or shuttle to the rooms to the left and right by clicking on the edges of the screen, or return to Overview by clicking near the top. Alt-Tab rolls you through the task list in each room, including the door icons, so you can both activate tasks and switch rooms that way too.

Simple, eh? Nothing like the power of a good metaphor and a clean, uncluttered implementation! Now all we have to do is make our own rooms, furnish them for *la vie electronique,* and get to work.

In Figure 3.3 I renamed Room 1 as Control Room. You can name or rename any room except Overlay and Overview. The only negative side effect with this invent-your-own naming is that rooms are ordered in the Overview alphabetically, so you either have to accept the floorplan that results from labeling rooms what you want or resort to tacking numbers in front of the names to make them appear in proper order. This is one of a number of flaws that pester an otherwise well-thought-out design.

I deleted the release notes icon and launched a copy of Windows Control Panel and the SYSEDIT utility from Program Manager—two programs I use constantly to fine-tune my machine. The act of invoking something through Progman from a Room installs an original instance of that object in that Room. Since Rooms installs Progman in the Overlay room, this places a Progman icon in every room, enabling you to conveniently launch applications while setting up additional rooms.

This is not the most efficient way to go about furnishing Rooms, however. While you have the option of simply leaving everything running in each room, this hogs resources, and eventually Windows will choke. In a truly object-oriented world, you would simply drag an icon off the

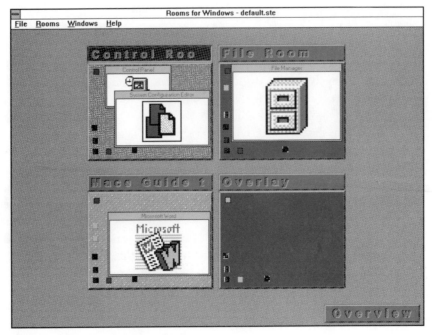

Figure 3.3   Renaming Room 1

Progman window into your room, and that would be that. It would not be running, it would just be there. Rooms doesn't go that far, but it offers an alternative form that works about as well.

When I created the Mace Guide to Windows room (Figure 3.3) for the purposes of writing this book, at first I used a copy of Word. But the book is actually composed of a number of files, and it made more sense to create "document buttons." To do this, you have to resort to the menu system. What menus, you say? The menus that you'll find attached to the backdoor icons (Figure 3.4). Stick with me, while I lead you into this labyrinth.

Now, there's nothing natural in assuming you should add an object to a Room by clicking on the back door (the escape hatch returning

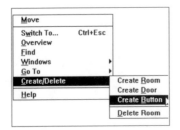

Figure 3.4   Creating "Document Buttons"

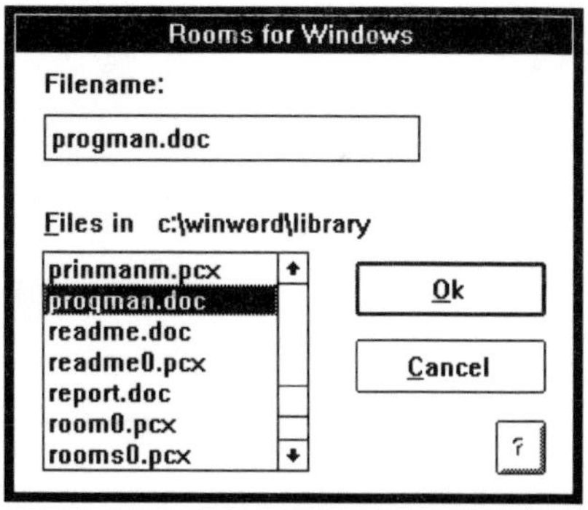

Figure 3.5   Using Windows' Browse

you from whence you came). Jeff regarded this as a tactical flaw. I agree, but, as I pointed out to him, the back door is the *only* piece of screen real estate guaranteed to be in every room. Another design quirk that could easily be cleaned up, no?

Like every menu system, this labyrinth leads eventually to the unremembered pathways of the DOS file system. If you don't happen to have all your files memorized, you'll encounter Windows' enfeebled version of the minotaur, Browse (Figure 3.5).

I don't know if Browse is meant to induce terminal bovine lethargy, or if it simply requires a cud chewer's patience. But I've grown accustomed to using it, even though I know perfectly well how to construct a DOS pathname. I'm just never certain what syntax each Windows application expects, so Browse I do, and let it digest what I pick, though it wastes time (Figure 3.6).

All of which, ultimately, produced this document button:  .

What are the benefits of this journey? The document button uses almost no system resources, and clicking on it launches Word with that particular file. Technically, this solution is not very intelligent. It works, but look at all the mess you have to contend with.

I also made a file room with a copy of File Manager running. That's the best you can do with Rooms regarding the file system, because it does not integrate file handling via drag-and-drop as Norton does.

Summary

My main gripes with Rooms have to do with poor quality control, as much as with the philosophical shortcomings I've talked about. Sometimes it's sloppy, and doesn't redraw the screen. Sometimes it wants extra

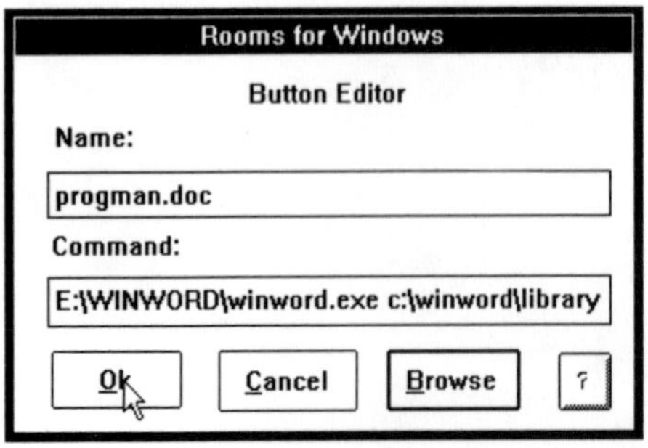

Figure 3.6 The result of using Browse

mouse clicks before it knows what you're pointing at. Sometimes it travels an extra room left or right or spontaneously drags an application from one room to the next—which is like being followed by a yappy dog. You can't get out of Rooms with applications open without feeding it file and pathnames. Oh, I'm sure in some instances I'm doing something wrong, I just have no idea what it is—and I'm a sophisticated computer user. If unwanted things happen to me, what about more ordinary mortals? But even Jeff believes the metaphor works well, as long as you don't crazy-glue yourself to absolute literalness in using it.

If it were technically difficult to cure these problems I would probably hush up, but they are the result of shortsighted design and sloppy programming—a genuine shame in a product of obvious merit from a company like Xerox.

If you are one who believes that given enough money and a good architect you would build a dream house with a perfect workspace for each aspect of your life, Rooms is for you.

4

Dashboard for Windows

Overview

The dashboard of your car is an area where, at a quick glance, you can absorb a lot of information and control everything that's worth controlling. Hewlett-Packard's Dashboard for Windows has created a utility as simple to use and as effective as its progenitor and namesake. The idea is to simplify what you need to work in Windows and put the essential controls within reach of a quick fingertip gesture. H-P unequivocally succeeds in combining utility, simplicity, and good aesthetics.

Details

The centerpiece of Dashboard is the windshield. As with XSoft Rooms, the best part of Dashboard, it is the simplest and easiest to explain (Figure 4.1).

Here I have Word running in the center of the windshield, and DOS running on the left. Double-clicking on any item, even the little dots that represent shrunken icons, takes you straight to them. You can also

Figure 4.1 Dashboard's windshield

rearrange the windshield by dragging and dropping items from one place to another.

This is really a series of miniature screens laid edge to edge—from three to nine of them, depending on your screen resolution and preferences. As you click on a panel or press the buttons beneath, Dashboard presents you with a new blank screen. You can launch new applications and arrange icons and windows in each of these screens. You can drag windows from one screen to another and move to that screen by clicking on the button at the bottom of it. Miniature versions of the full screen that identify themselves with text will appear in the Dashboard windshield. You can move anywhere by simply pointing and clicking.

Philosophically, Dashboard is futuristic and minimalist, the universe condensed into one small instrument panel. By simply pointing to something, you can see more. Otherwise, it remains unobtrusively available. When you think of the sprawling layers of mess that compose Program Manager, it's amazing that the same information can be organized so economically (Figure 4.2).

DASHBOARD INSTRUMENTATION

A tour of Dashboard's instruments follows.

Quit, Launch, Save Configuration

We have the usual Windows single bar in the upper-left side of the Dashboard. Next to it is a double bar, which gives you a "launch" menu. This is the equivalent of double-clicking on any of the icons. These menus should all be considered part of the keyboard interface for those who don't have a mouse or don't like taking their hands off the keys (Figure 4.3). It also serves when icons disappear under other windows. Third in line is a `save configuration` icon for Dashboard itself.

Shrink, Iconize, Maximize

To the right of the title bar is the double-down arrow button. Pressing this button removes the strip of Windows groups you can access, in

Figure 4.2 Dashboard's economic organization

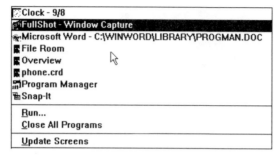

Figure 4.3 The launch menu

exchange for a slightly narrower, space-conserving, aerodynamic dashboard. Look at one example to see the difference—first, the full Dashboard (Figure 4.4).

Pressing the double-down arrow gives you the even-slimmer version, a veritable fashion model of a control panel (Figure 4.5).

Even the larger of the two options is fairly small, but if you choose a default setting that keeps the Dashboard floating above all other windows (even the active one), the thinner option may help conserve space. This set of controls also includes the usual Windows maximize-minimize buttons.

GROUP BUTTONS

Notice that below the title bar all my Windows groups have been turned into buttons below the title bar (Figure 4.6). Click on one and a list drops down, giving you both a look and the chance to launch an application. Here's the Main group in Figure 4.7.

Notice you can open the group window as you would in Program Manager, though I can't imagine a practical reason why. In fact, one drawback to Dashboard concerns modifying the default paths of the objects. If you move something to a new subdirectory, you will have to run Progman to set new properties, then have Dashboard re-read the Progman Group settings.

Figure 4.4 The full Dashboard

Figure 4.5   The slimmed-down version of Dashboard

 Quick Launch

To the left of the windshield are the "quick launch" icons. File Manager is a default installation. I deleted Windows Write, which Setup put there, and added instead the escape-to-DOS prompt. I'll cover how that, and other customization, is done farther on, but you can have multiple launch icons here—you'll get scroll arrows when you do.

And, of course, for those who live by it, there's a clock, here customized to appear "analog" in intaglio. The product will let you customize your dash by choosing from a range of analog and digital clocks.

 **System Information and Configuration**

To the right of the Windshield, the fuel gauge is watching Windows memory usage and reporting current resource use. This will make apparent to you the consequences of having a lot of different applications running at once. You can watch the fuel gauge drop dramatically as you launch new programs. Double-click on the fuel gauge and all sorts of other statistics about the beast's digital metabolism can be revealed.

Figure 4.8 represents what you get after double-clicking on the fuel gauge: the System Resources report window. Notice there are other windows you can access from here: System Environment, Drive Usage, Applications Running, and Environment Variables.

System Environment gives you a quick overview of what hardware and drivers you have installed (like Norton's System Info). Drive Usage lets you know what size your logical disk drives are and how much space on them you have available. The Applications Running report window tells you what apps are currently running and how much memory they're using. The Environment Variables report window won't be

Figure 4.6   Windows groups become buttons

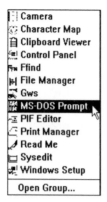

Figure 4.7   The Main group

useful to too many users, but it will be very useful to those who are advanced enough to use DOS' environment variables; it reports all the stored environment arguments.

 **Printer Status and Configuration**

The printer button shows the current printers that Windows has set up for use. There is also a small "LED" indicator that shows which one is currently getting printer output. The size of this display is contingent on how many printers you have installed and how much room Dashboard has to display them.

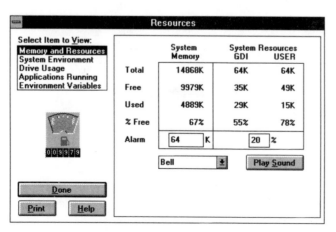

Figure 4.8   The Systems Resources report window

Help, Customize, About

The "?" is, unremarkably, for Help, but the way it functions is clever and ought to be universally adopted: Click on the "?" with the mouse and you pick up the question mark. You can now drag and drop it onto the screen object that has you puzzled. Help pops up in the proper context with information on that item. Yes!

The wrench is less obvious. It means "customize." Double-click on it and you get the screen in Figure 4.9.

Here, I've deleted the Write icon from the quick launch area, and I'm ready to add an MS-DOS icon for escape to DOS.

You can also rearrange where the various controls appear on the dashboard or hide things or make several other adjustments to suit your needs and tastes. Some of these are minor advantages, such as selectable clock faces, but others such as the left-to-right order of display make Dashboard customizable in a truly productive way.

The HP logo below the wrench icon is the "about" button.

Summary

Don't let the brevity of the review fool you: This is my favorite. Buy this product.

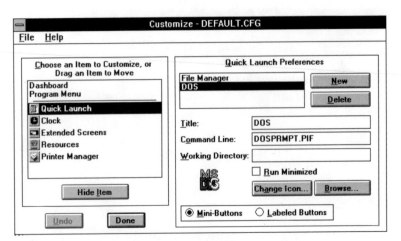

Figure 4.9 The customize screen

5

Squeegee

Overview

A simple, powerful Program Manager alternative, Squeegee from
ICOM Simulations follows the Windows philosophy of menus and hot
keys, but packs them all under a single icon that follows you every-
where, offering instant, compact access. Like an actual squeegee, this
product aims to clean up your windows.

Details

ICOM's claim on the package is "Bypass Program Manager." Squeegee,
however, doesn't substitute itself for Progman. What it does is drop a
Squeegee icon onto the title bar of the *active* window next to the control
button.

No matter where you go in Windows, this piece of programming cleverness will keep the Squeegee in sight at all times in the upper-left corner of the active window. Hence, the logic flows, you will never need to
return to Progman to find, launch, or manipulate files; just click on the
squeegee, and *voila!*

Squeegee offers you a pull-down menu that includes configuration
options, all your program groups, and their contents (Figure 5.1). Beats
tracking down a deeply buried Progman icon by a mile.

59

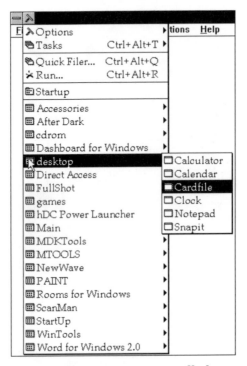

Figure 5.1   Squeegee's pull-down menu

You can sort this list, you can add dividers (which are visual indicators used to group menu items according to your preference), and subsort within these categories. You can add new items you want to access directly, such as programs or files, or new groups. This all happens in a straightforward, Windows-like fashion, so I won't detail the process here.

By way of example, though, let me show another Squeegee feature, the Project in Figure 5.2.

It's a straight shot through the Options|Configuration menu to the Project selection. What we're creating here is a new menu item with a special attribute: the ability to launch multiple programs with a simple mouse-click or hot-key combo (Figure 5.3).

You give the Project a name and press the key combination, if any, you want to use to launch it. Click OK and we're back at the Configuration menu, where we will add pieces to our project.

In Figure 5.4 I've looked up two word processing files in the directory on the left and installed them in the Book Project on the right. I'm about to select a third document, Win31.DOC, and install it.

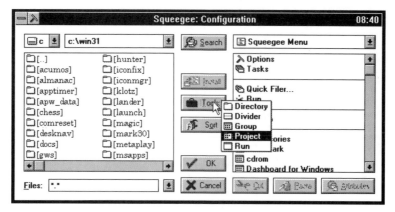

Figure 5.2 Selecting the Project feature from the Configuration menu

Now, when I pull down the main menu, there is a new item listed, "Book," along with its hot-key. Under it is a sub-menu listing the contents of my Project. I can launch the pieces one at a time or simply double-click on Book (or use the hot-key combo), and Squeegee launches all files and required applications.

Of course there are a couple of basic Windows assumptions under all this. Data files must be associated with executable programs for this auto-launch business to work. But Squeegee lets you establish or modify such things directly, associating .DOC files, for instance, with Word for Windows (Figure 5.5).

Inherent in Squeegee is its own file manager. I found the Quick Filer, as it's called, more straightforward and powerful than the native Windows File Manager. It's best feature is an enhanced Search facility that lets you locate files based on a number of different criteria, including embedded text strings, and then launch them immediately.

The Quick Filer has two basic windows, both available all the time. One is a one-directory list (Figure 5.6), the other a two-directory list, which takes more screen real estate and lets you work files back and forth from one place to another.

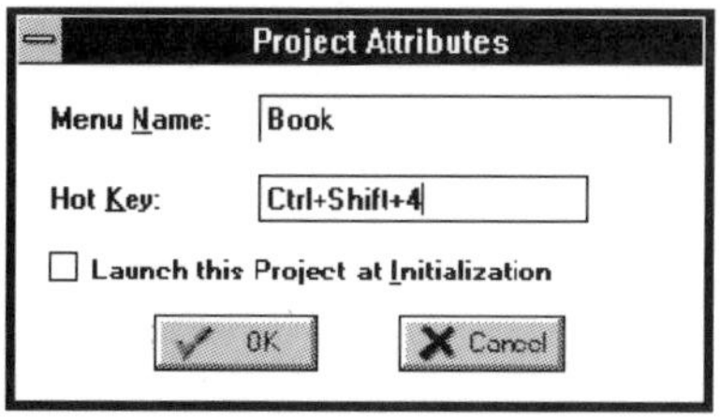

Figure 5.3 Creating a new menu item

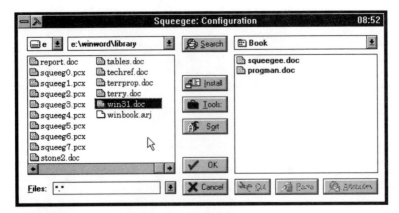

Figure 5.4   Installing files in the Project Book

Once you select a file or set of files in the directory display, you can execute any of the appropriate functions represented by the push buttons on the left (logically, you can run, but not edit .EXEs, and edit, but not run .INIs).

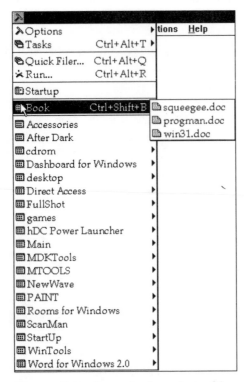

Figure 5.5   Associating data files with programs

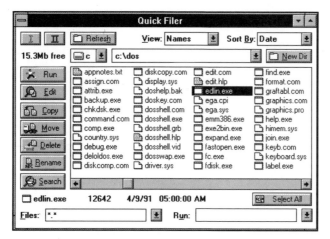

Figure 5.6   Quick Filer's one-directory list

The editor that the edit key brings up is Notepad, by the way, even if the selected file is written in a proper word processor's format. Some people might find that a defect, but Jeff, for one, considers it a less time-consuming choice, since Notepad loads more quickly than most proper word processors.

A small benefit worth mentioning is the icons used for those functions: They actually bear some resemblance to the thing they signify.

Quick Filer also gives you access to the squeegee and the current time, as well as file information, if you've selected anything. You reach the two-directory configuration by pressing the Ⅱ button.

Figure 5.7 shows a more appetizing setup for copying and moving files, but uses more screen space.

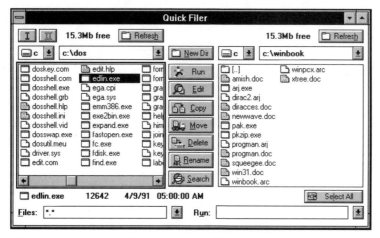

Figure 5.7   Two-directory configuration

❏ *Icons*

An icon *is* a sign. Unlike its grownup, complex sister—the symbol, which is a thing of great and wondrous meaning—a sign has one and only one interpretation:

For instance, 🛑 means stop.

Now, admittedly, most signs are culture bound—the two-fingered "peace" sign to an American means "up yours" to an Australian. There is even a philosophical discipline associated with their study—Semiotics, invented by Frenchman, author, and thinker, the late Roland Barthes.

But even before Barthes, humans had long specialized in the art and craft of signs; we call such people designers (de-signers). While we tend to think of them categorically as those who specialize in drawing things such as office buildings, clothing, or sports cars, they are, in fact, general masters at representing images and ideas exactly by means of line, color, and space. Good designers create unambiguous images, images which mean one thing and one thing only. For if not, the architect's building could not be raised in steel and stone, the couturier's clothing could never be cut and sewn, nor Corvettes molded and assembled, for the endless bickering of those who do the work over the meaning and intent of the master drawings. The beauty of a good design is that we get it.

What does this have to do with Windows utilities? Well, after using over a hundred new Windows programs and ten thousand icons in less than six months, Jeff and I mostly didn't get it. So don't be surprised if you mostly don't either.

We are appalled at the utter lack of awareness on the part of software developers for basic good design. Rather, we think they all fancy themselves designers at heart and can't resist exposing the rest of us to their craft. Now it is true that even Microsoft took five or six years before hiring someone who knew more or less what they were doing to design the Windows screens and icons. I think they were last employed designing TV game shows, but still, they show some accomplishment at the art. We're always inclined to show tolerance for juvenile efforts by smaller companies. But come on, guys; even in a small town such as mine there are three or four talented designers who work for considerably less than average programmers. It's time to wake up and recognize that in Windows (or any graphical based system) the design is as important as the code. Poor design is just as crippling as slow or buggy code—and you, the user, should complain about it as loudly as you would if the software crashed your machine or was dog slow.

Poor design, juvenile artwork, incomprehensible layout, and enigmatic icons destined one day to drive some digital archaeologist mataglap make your life harder and your workday less productive. Pray these same people are never commissioned to do the bathroom signs in some large airport.

A good icon is worth a thousand words typed on the command line. A bad icon is a sinkhole of confusion!

Summary

While other programs offer similar features, Squeegee is best at integrating Program Manager features without altering the basic design philosophy of Windows. You get enhanced program and file management all folded neatly under a single, ever-present icon. Extended powers are offered to organize and launch projects consisting of many files. This is my idea of a great utility: It's designed do one thing better, and it succeeds.

Squeegee is best for people who aren't looking to change the basic Windows style, but prefer a more compact approach to Program Manager and a more logical approach to File Manager. It's less compelling for folks who have mastered the intricacies of those pesky Managers and don't want the overhead of adapting to a different, but superior, form.

Amish Utilities for Windows

Overview

There's something very interesting about The Amish Utilities for Windows from Amish Software. They're packaged very much like Golden Age of DOS utilities. There are six little pieces (the rule that six items are about all that most people can memorize holds well here), each of which you can use alone, and each of which serves a useful function that many, but not all, people will want.

Details

The installation is completely elementary. The result doesn't do anything complicated or hard to find. It installs one group with six programs (Figure 6.1).

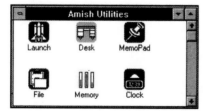

Figure 6.1 One group with six programs

THE UTILITIES

 Launch

Amish's Launch utility is a way to reorganize your Program Manager interface. The idea of Launch is to have quick access to the most important items you need, escaping from the *Concentration* game of having to remember where your applications and files are.

You trigger Launch's menu with keyboard hot-keys—the default is the Word Perfect-like `Ctrl-Alt-L`, although, blessedly, you can change it. You can also invoke the menu by pressing the left mouse button anywhere on the desktop. Depending on what else you have running, this may or may not work.

Launch's default arrangement is to have a menu item for each group, with a cascaded entry for each item within that group.

Amish also assumes you'll want access to the Program Manager from wherever you are, as well as the ability to shell out to DOS. They give you the chance to tile all your open windows or cascade them. Launch's default gives you access to the Task Manager.

Of course, these choices are only the defaults. Amish allows for a great deal of customization of what applications to include, in what order they appear, and what hot-keys you use to access them. You customize Launch by selecting the first item on the default Launch menu, `Configure Amish Launch`. Selecting that choice brings up a configuration screen (Figure 6.2).

The `Installation` choice allows three options for Launch: making it the default Windows shell, "overriding" Program Manager; executing at the beginning of a Windows session, but not "overriding" Program Manager; or not loading it but having it accessible. The `Hotkey`

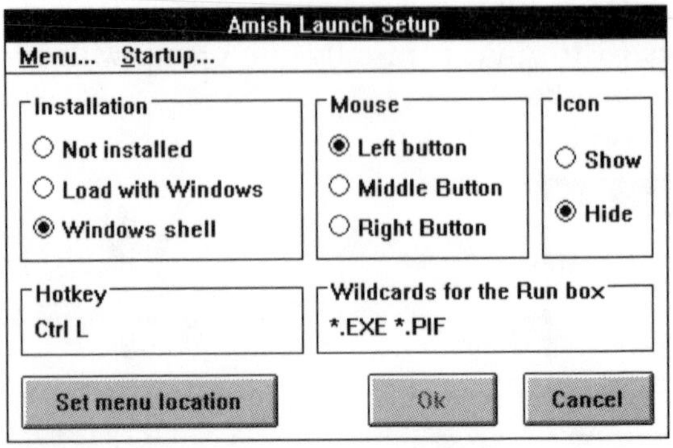

Figure 6.2 Customizing launch

Figure 6.3   Big OK button

specification allows you to override the default and replace it. You can also change which mouse button press brings up (or doesn't—this feature doesn't work consistently) the Launch menu. You set up the location where the Launch menu appears with the Set menu location window, which you drag to the location you want to specify and then press on the largest OK button in the history of Western Civilization (Figure 6.3)

Launch is useful, especially for those of you who are keyboard-oriented. It overcomes much of the *Concentration* memory game nightmare. It allows you quick access to your most frequently used files. It's simple, adds some value, and doesn't take up a lot of memory, so if you run it in lieu of Program Manager, it may help performance. Jeff's bias toward simplicity made him like Launch, but I thought they might have overshot the simplicity model. There's no law saying they couldn't add some value and features to it.

 Desk

Amish Desk is a program that provides you with numerous multiple "screens." For people who run more than one program during the day, and especially for those who run more than one program at once, virtual screens allow you to see all of them without minimizing any of them. Here's how it works. First, you double-click on the Desk icon, and it brings up the Desk window.

This Tic-Tac-Toe emulator is something you'll encounter in several Windows products. It offers nine of what are known as "virtual" screens; imagine what you see on your monitor is merely one area of a larger matrix. In this case, it's three-by-three, each displaying one, or several, applications. The Desk in Figure 6.4 shows a maximized Program Manager and an icon in the upper left, with the other eight screens empty. With only one application open, the value added by Desk isn't very obvious. But put another program up, for example Word, (Figure 6.5).

Figure 6.4 The Desk window

Here's a typical, multiple, overlapping window display. But Word really requires almost all of the screen to make working in it acceptable, and Program Manager is not much different. With virtual screens, you can click on one of these mini-windows, and, without minimizing it, drag it to another "screen." The result looks like Figure 6.6.

Now you can move from program to program without constantly minimizing, simply by using the right mouse button to click on one of the other virtual screens. Sure, you can do this in Windows with the Task Manager or the Alt-Tab key routine, but that means resorting to menus or consulting that great virtual screen between your ears. If you actually want to *see* where you're going, this is the better way.

Desk is highly customizable. The control menu of the window brings up the Amish Desk Options screen, which is where you tweak Desk's workings (Figure 6.7).

You can keep the virtual screen display on top of active windows, keep the little representative image updated or not, or organize windows to a logical grid. You can change the three-by-three display arrangement and have up to eight cells in either direction. Anyone who uses eight screens by eight, in my opinion, is a self-indulgent geek or is doing a very specialized kind of work. There are other options, too: You can display the representations of programs as windows with title bars or as icons or both. You can also dictate what happens to all these scattered windows if you exit Desk.

Desk is useful for users who run lots of things and need them to be maximized to be productive. The implementation is smooth and logical,

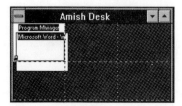

Figure 6.5 Two open applications

Figure 6.6 Making it tidy

down to the pleasant title bar hints that tell you what you're moving when you're moving a window. The design is more than adequate for the useful job it performs.

 Memo Pad

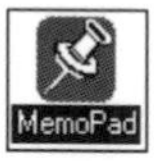

Amish Utilities' Memo Pad program aims to replace the blizzard of Post-It Notes that adorn most people's work areas. Additionally, you can do some things with Memo Pad you can't with physical paper notes. You can organize notes by category, find a note, even in a big pile, based on content, or have an Alarm Note, that is, a Post-It that rings at you and pops up at a specified time.

When you click on Memo Pad, it behaves like many DOS utilities—it doesn't do anything right away. It will (if configured that way) display

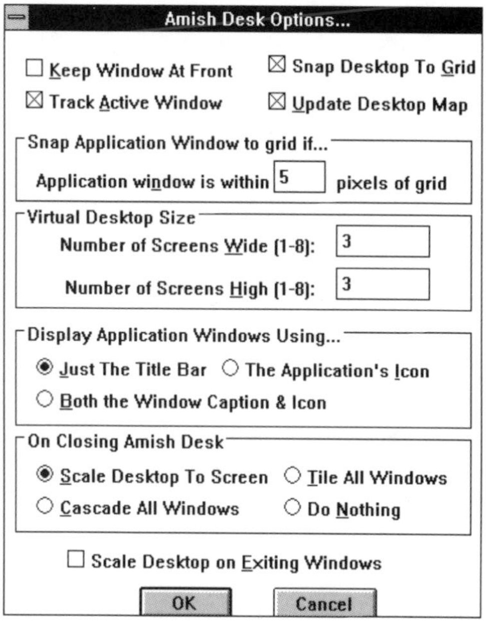

Amish Desk Options...

☐ Keep Window At Front   ☒ Snap Desktop To Grid
☒ Track Active Window   ☒ Update Desktop Map

Snap Application Window to grid if...
Application window is within [5]   pixels of grid

Virtual Desktop Size
Number of Screens Wide (1-8): [3]
Number of Screens High (1-8): [3]

Display Application Windows Using...
◉ Just The Title Bar   ○ The Application's Icon
○ Both the Window Caption & Icon

On Closing Amish Desk
◉ Scale Desktop To Screen   ○ Tile All Windows
○ Cascade All Windows   ○ Do Nothing

☐ Scale Desktop on Exiting Windows

[OK]   [Cancel]

Figure 6.7 Tweaking Desk's options

the program's icon. If you click on the icon, it brings up all its controls, and these are a mite confusing.

There's a main `Control Panel` and a `Configure` choice, and both have configuration options. They allow you to print a deck of notes, set up a basic size and color scheme, save to disk, pick fonts, and decide whether or not to display the button bar on the memos.

When you get a memo up (either by picking `Create` a note off the Memo Pad menu, or pressing the intuitively non-obvious `Shift-Alt-D`, or by double-clicking with the left mouse button on the program icon), you can type in as much as you want, and, unlike a paper Post-It Note, the text will continue to scroll. There are editing features, albeit limited ones beyond wrap and scrolling, that you reach through a button bar.

Memo Pad Tools

Memo Pad offers the following controls: cut selected text, paste, copy, copy all (the contents of the note), time/date stamp, and open the Memo Pad control panel.

You can print one or all notes or search for specific contents.

Memo Pad supports multiple "layouts," that is, groups of notes. This a logical way to categorize your Post-It Notes. You can have a memo in one or more layouts, hide any or all layouts, or show them all.

Memo Pad is a pared-down, little note-filing utility, neither as complex nor as well-rounded as dedicated note-tracking products such as Micro Logic's Info Select. Like Launch, it's tidy and good enough to work, but not likely to dazzle.

 ### File

The most useful utility in the Amish package is File. It's the most complex of the Amish programs, but it also the one that most ameliorates Windows' shortcomings. If you double-click on the File icon, you get to the Amish File window (Figure 6.8).

This extremely sensible window, while quite large, presents all the necessary tools for flat file management. There are the obvious controls for specifying drive and directory, and a convenient `System Stats` display that gives you the kind of information you get from the **DOS** CHKDSK command, with the addition of the `Free Resource` data you need as a Windows user.

What makes Amish File such a winner are functions you could always get in a good DOS shell, such as PC Tools, but with the additional

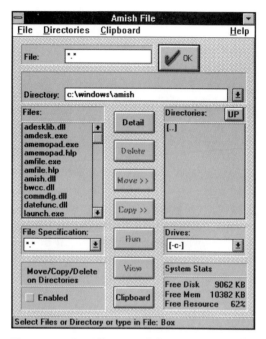

Figure 6.8 File, Amish's most useful utility

simplicity and cleanliness of good graphical user interface design. There are well-placed buttons for delete, move, and copy functions. Just click on a file or files, press the appropriate button, and whoosh, it works. Delete is very powerful, maybe too powerful. You can delete an entire directory and all the files in it, as well as all the subdirectories underneath it, contents and all, depending on the way you've set up your options in the `File Manipulation Options` window called from the Amish File menu bar (Figure 6.9).

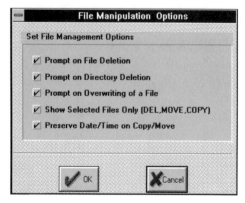

Figure 6.9 Selecting options

Amish is basically giving you permission to purposefully (or accidentally) have the root as your current directory, mark it for deletion, and, if you don't have the "Prompt on Directory Deletion" box checked, wipe out a whole drive. They warn you in the documentation that this is possible (I checked), but this feature seems tantamount to arming a random sample of 100,000 people with loaded automatic weapons, each of which carries a warning label not to discharge in school playgrounds. That is to say, they've *said* the responsible thing, but truly awful things can still result.

Except for this dangerous possibility, I'd say if the default Windows File Manager had been written by skilled software designers, it would have come out something like Amish File.

The window also has buttons for Run (running a selected file), View (viewing the selected file, which works for some things but not others), and Clipboard. Clipboard brings up a stack (a most-recent-on-top pile) of the items stored by user editing actions to the Clipboard. You can view and even edit these.

You can get more detail in your file listing by pressing the Detail button, bringing up the Amish File Detail window (Figure 6.10).

You can color-code or highlight files by their attributes, and within this window, you can change the file attributes of listed items. The Detail HiLight window holds the controls for these functions (Figure 6.11).

You can mark files for highlighting in specific colors based on age (new, old, or both, as you define the terms), their file attributes (Archive, Systems, Hidden, Read-Only), and whether those files are "large" or "medium" (again, as you define the terms). This latter file size feature is especially useful when you're looking to make room on your hard disk for those space-hungry Windows programs, and need to clear off old or big files. You can also sort by the usual suspects: date, size, alpha, or file type.

Amish File Detail - c:\windows\amish*.*				
File	Display	Attributes		Help
amish.dll	A	04/01/1992	01:03:00	58640 Bytes
bwcc.dll	A	04/01/1992	01:03:00	124304 Bytes
launch.exe	A	04/01/1992	01:03:00	9726 Bytes
isetup.exe	A	04/01/1992	01:03:00	12456 Bytes
amdesk.exe	A	04/01/1992	01:03:00	85776 Bytes
adesklib.dll	A	04/01/1992	01:03:00	3264 Bytes
amemopad.exe	A	04/01/1992	01:03:00	75264 Bytes
amemopad.hlp	A	04/01/1992	01:03:00	46053 Bytes
amfile.exe	A	04/01/1992	01:03:00	152174 Bytes
amfile.hlp	A	04/01/1992	01:03:00	44171 Bytes
commdlg.dll	A	04/01/1992	01:03:00	89248 Bytes

Figure 6.10 The Amish File Detail

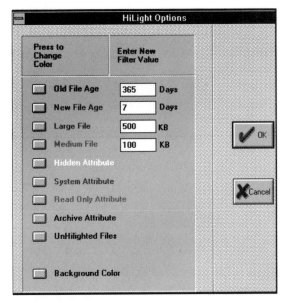

Figure 6.11   Controls for file attributes

File's displays in these areas are not only attractive but get top honors for effectiveness, if you're not into system speed, which you clearly aren't or you wouldn't be messing around with Windows. We should mention here that Amish File seems really slow to anyone who used any of the old PC Tools–type DOS shells, but barring speed as a consideration, this is a strong entry for File Manager enhancement champion.

 Memory

Double-clicking on the program creates a subtle, but fairly useful window letting you know how much memory you have available. You might not even see it if your screen is busy enough or it comes up on one of your virtual screens ▣ 10,408 .

Amish Memory does a lot more than this, though. Amazingly enough, the `Preferences` window for this utility is large enough for Brobidnagians to play lacrosse on (Figure 6.12).

You can specify a broad range of options, from what to display in the Lilliputian memory window to how precisely to display it. Memory will alert you to low-memory conditions in RAM, disk space, or system resources, all based on how you define low memory.

While Memory is tidy and useful, it also reminds you of the main reason utilities exist: the weakness of operating system software. Microsoft, in its infinite wisdom, created an operating environment

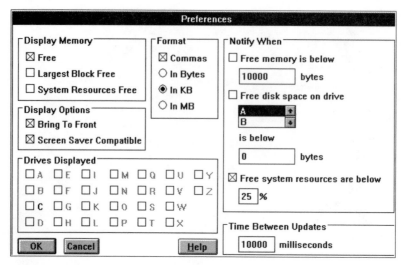

Figure 6.12 Specifying preferences for Memory

with a teenage appetite for resources. The software has outrun the normal hardware's ability. Amish's Memory utility is a melancholic reminder of this frail pairing of greedy system software and the mortal coil of contemporary Intel boxes of less than 486 pedigree.

 Clock

Clock, uninterestingly enough, takes Windows' default clock displays and advances them to the next level. It has some useful functions, to whit: alarms to prompt you, hourly beeps *à la* digital watches, alarms that set off programs, stop watches, and countdown timers (reverse stop watches). The default screen shows the current time and date.

Again, the Preferences screen for this program is about 130 times the size of the program's screen (Figure 6.13).

You can dictate the way hours, days, months, and years appear. You can pick date formats. You can describe the screen location for the little chrono-window, how it displays, and how to handle Clock events if you're in a DOS box when one happens. Clock, especially for you Chronos fans, is a useful little utility, not alone worth the price of the package, but not without merit to many people.

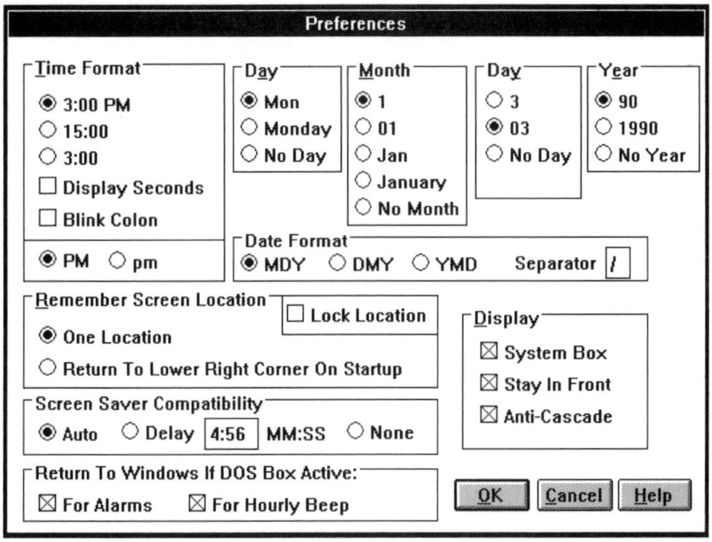

Figure 6.13   Specifying preferences for time/date

Summary

The Amish Utilities, with the exception of File, are slight improvements to Windows. None, with the exception of File, is worth the expense of the package. File, while an outstanding example of good design, is slower than Robert Dole's hand jive beat. Yet, all together, it adds enough value and productivity to various pieces of Windows that most people would find it worth the price tag.

7

Task Manager

Overview

Metz bills Task Manager as "The simple solution for Microsoft Windows task and file management." A modest claim, but perhaps the hardest to completely fulfill. Simplicity does not come easy or without a price.

Details

This product's abilities are in two areas: Task management (launching) and file management.

TASK MANAGER

The main TaskMan window certainly advances toward the first goal of Progman replacement by saving room on screen (Figure 7.1). Here we have all the essentials: a list of currently executing programs displayed in a window for selection, and a handful of vital file handling functions gathered as buttons along the top. Together, they satisfy the second requirement of a useful Progman replacement, to integrate file and task management.

Once launched, TaskMan lurks in a hidden window. Unless you set a Preference for the program to "stay visible," it is not listed in the Windows queue of tasks, so Alt-Tab won't get you there. Instead you

Figure 7.1   A useful Progman replacement

press `Ctrl-Esc`. Simple enough once you know the trick. Now you can switch to the application you want by clicking on it, or use the Launch/Remove icons.

 Launch/Remove

The top button launches the selected application full-screen. The bottom one removes an executing task. If you want to find a new application to launch, click on the down arrow to the right of the Task List (Figure 7.2).

This drops a list of all Windows applications groups. Select one and you'll get a view of the contents, ready for launch (Figure 7.3).

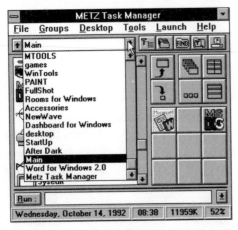

Figure 7.2   Selecting the Main group

Figure 7.3 Opening the Main group

One special feature here: You'll notice above the Word for Windows and MS-DOS logos on the matrix of buttons on TaskMan's right, what they call the "launch pad." These are quick-launch buttons, and while there are menu options for defining them, the simplest method is to drag and drop an icon from the Groups window onto a blank button. If you want to further modify the selection, click on it with the right mouse button and customize launch parameters. Customization includes naming a specific data file, creating a default working directory for the application, and deciding whether the invoked application will start running normal, minimized, maximized, or hidden.

 Full-Screen/Minimized

For applications that are not currently running, the options are "launch full-screen" and "launch minimized," as an icon. It's worth repeating that within the menu system there are options for fully customizing the launch parameters. While powerful, that process in Windows is not so simple. TaskMan, to its credit, makes it *possible*; it does nothing to make it easy.

 **Run**

The Run feature completes the visible task management options. This is similar to the Windows File|Run menu selection (TaskMan has that option as well) for launching applications whose file name you know and love to type. It adds an arrow on the right, however, that drops a list of all the previous Run commands you've issued—the Windows equivalent of DOS history utilities like DOSEDIT. Obviously, this is extremely handy for those people who loop through the same commands over and over again, or with slight variation.

FILE MANAGEMENT FEATURES

File management is integrated through a toolbar at the top right of the screen. But it's very basic and oddly disjointed.

Directory Tree

First up is a directory tree button. I couldn't figure out why this was separated from the file selector. Is some deep-seated DOS heritage showing through? Why aren't files and directories more closely entwined? In any case, this button functions like the change directory command in DOS.

This window (Figure 7.4) allows you to either use the mouse to traverse up and down directory hierarchies or directly type in what you want. There are a pair of ambiguously labeled buttons at the bottom of the window, Change and Select. An irritating interface blemish is here, waiting to pop up like some adolescent's blackhead. The (highlighted) default button here is Change, so Jeff assumed this meant "Change the current directory to directory you have selected," and that the Select button meant "Select a new one." He thought this not because of the words, but because of TaskMan's default choice. He was wrong. The default choice sets you up to change what's entered, so

Figure 7.4 Directory tree screen

typing in your new directory and pressing return doesn't save that as your choice and pop you back out, the way most Windows dialog boxes work; it just leaves you in the window, waiting for you to change the named subdirectory. You can escape from here only with your mouse.

File Select

Once you've gotten the right directory with the tree button and mastered the escape, you can use the `File Select` button to actually select something.

Here we have all the basic file management maneuvers: Copy, Move, Rename, Launch, Print, and Delete (Figure 7.5). Blessedly, drag-and-drop is fully implemented, so you can select a file or files with the mouse and, holding down the left button, drag an icon to the button that represents the operation you want performed. When you release the mouse button, the program performs the operation on the selected files.

One drawback here is that selecting the source and destination files requires you to know the full DOS pathname. There is no Browse option as in most Windows file handlers, and this is going to stop some people cold. This is not fatal, but it's a completely ridiculous omission. The Browse function is almost universal within Windows applications that require you to know the data file. The code for it is trivial, far easier than many of the things Metz has accomplished here.

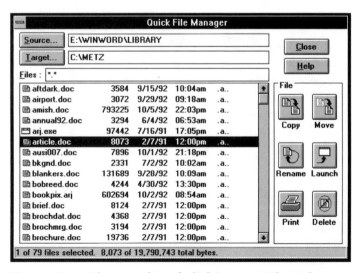

Figure 7.5 The results of clicking on File Select

Find

The File Finder is rudimentary. It only searches for files based on their names; it will not search for text strings within files. For that you must use the next icon.

Text Search

This is the text search button, and it basically looks through files for matching ASCII text.

System Status

Last, there's the system status button. It reveals basic statistics about your machine and drive storage capacity and lets you edit the critical system files, should you be so bold (Figure 7.6).

I'm tempted to describe Task Manager as simplistic. I suppose the idea was to break everything down into operations so elemental no one could screw up. The result is to make life more difficult because no one tool does completely what the user needs. That and the DOS-like requirement for path names cripple file operations in Task Manager.

OTHER FUNCTIONS

There are other things of note in this package. Let's begin with those other icons in Task Manager.

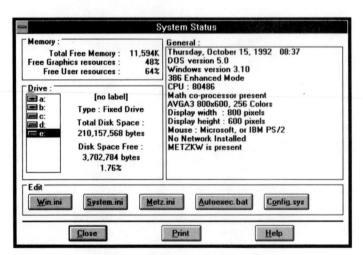

Figure 7.6 System Status reveals stats and storage

Cascade/Overlap

These allow you to quickly reorganize the screen as cascading, overlapping, or stacked windows, or to rearrange the icons. Underneath these choices, in the File Preferences menu, lie the tools for modestly customizing the behavior of Task Manager.

 Scheduler

The package includes a Scheduler, which is not part of Task Manager, but can be run separately or loaded onto a blank launch pad button. With this you can set applications to launch at a particular date and time. This might be useful for remote communications, but you will have to master Windows Recorder or an equivalent utility to get real use of this feature. After all, a program must do more than sit there.

The package also includes a separate program called Launch that lets you customize the Launch menu in Task Manager or attach selected programs to the Windows File Manager menu system—a sort of backwards approach to integrating file handling and program management.

Summary

I have decidedly mixed thoughts about this package. Simplicity is a virtue, and so is individuality. Metz Task Manager has both. But at what point does individuality degrade the unwritten rules of conduct and at what point does simplicity lapse into stupidity? The basic program and file management functions of Task Manager are what Metz claims, simpler and more straightforward than Program Manager. The Launch buttons are well-located, compact, and self-evident.

But the file handling aspects are overly simplified and retain vestigial DOS qualities—such as requiring you to know and be able to construct full path names, something Windows was supposed to free users from.

Novice Windows users are going to like much of Task Manager, but they will stumble in mastering some file handling features. Once you enter the menu system, confusion will abound, with many murkily named options and lots of choices that contribute only marginally to the usefulness of the software. People who are comfortable in a DOS environment, pathnames and all, can get good use out of the atomic file tools and the truly useful launch buttons.

For everyone else, Task Manager is probably worthwhile owning for the task management tools, while you'll need to fall back on File Manager or something better for file handling and wait for Metz's next and, I trust, improved version.

8

Trailblazer 1.1

Overview

Trailblazer is a Program Manager/File Manager replacement with a strong and unusual point of view. Aesthetically pleasing and adorned with little humanizing touches, Trailblazer is loaded with function and virtue, but the Twisted Pine folk clearly have their own, sometimes impenetrable, idea of interface in the functional as well as the aesthetic sense.

Details

If you install the product as your default shell, Windows brings up a solitary screen when you activate it (Figure 8.1).

The design is very trim; there are no menu choices. The Twisted Pine folk describe the screen as granite, and the component windows as "slates." The granite has a highly lithological look to it.

IBM declared Common User Access as a way to make all software alike as a productivity boost. This meant surrender of truly awful, truly brilliant, or just truly different ways of doing things in favor of worshipping at the Temple of the Big Blue Mean. Before we blaze any trails, there's an important fact to note about this beautiful and innovative product, what I've called its *Un*common User Access (UUA) approach to interface. The Twisted Pine folk are at least one standard deviation

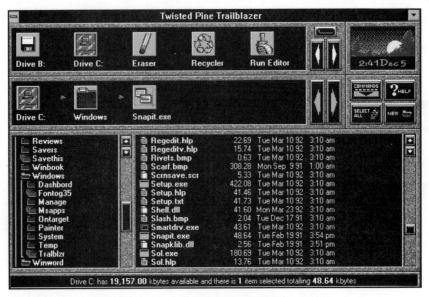

Figure 8.1   Trailblazer as default shell

away from conforming to the CUA/Windows way of doing things. While their view has some benefits, and some deficits (as we describe in the following pages), it is definitely a view all their own, highly flavored and distinctive.

TREE VIEW SLATE

Trailblazer's file management capabilities are built around a pair of adjacent slates. The first is the `Tree View` slate in Figure 8.2.

When you first bring up the screen, there's only a listing of root subdirectories. But notice some of the folders that represent a subdirectory have an icon with one file, while others have several. This is the Trailblazer way of letting you know which subdirectories have their

Figure 8.2   Listing of root subdirectories

**Figure 8.3   Listing of subdirectories'
subdirectories**

own subdirectories. Click on one of those multi-folder choices, and it unfolds that part of the directory tree (Figure 8.3). Note the nonconformist slider bar at the right of this window. The arrow keys are together at the top, which makes sense. It's useful to have the controls together so if you overshoot it's a quick click back.

FILE VIEW SLATE

If you single-click again on a subdirectory, it folds the tree up. If you single-click on a single-folder subdirectory, nothing happens, an unusual interface twist. This when paired with another unusual one—the fact that arrow keys don't let you navigate these lists—is disconcerting, because virtually all the other Windows utilities let you move through lists with arrow keys. *Double*-clicking on a subdirectory brings up a file listing in the `View` Slate, just to the right of the `Tree View` Slate (Figure 8.4).

The `View` slate lets you double-click on files to launch them and their related applications. Trailblazer features drag-and-drop functions, but you can't drag from this particular slate, another surprise. There is some ability to customize in the `View` slate. For example, you can tell Trailblazer to give you a List Box view, which gives you access to multiple layers of hierarchical directories. This is very valuable for people

Auntjudy.fog	27.22	Sun Aug 23 92 12:13 pm
Civitype.fog	67.08	Sun Aug 23 92 12:14 pm
Firi____.afm	18.10	Sun Aug 23 92 12:32 pm
Firi____.cfg	0.51	Sun Aug 23 92 12:32 pm
Firi____.inf	0.54	Sun Aug 23 92 12:32 pm
Firi____.pfb	11.16	Sun Aug 23 92 12:32 pm
Firi____.pfm	5.10	Sun Aug 23 92 12:32 pm
Fontinfo.txt	16.67	Tue Aug 18 92 10:56 am
Froman.fog	30.05	Sun Aug 23 92 12:14 pm
Fromita.fog	35.53	Sun Aug 23 92 12:14 pm
Fromita.fon	12.26	Sun Aug 23 92 12:33 pm
Fromita.ttf	24.85	Sun Aug 23 92 12:33 pm
Gcitymod.fog	114.78	Sun Aug 23 92 12:13 pm
Goudyhun.fog	60.94	Sun Aug 23 92 12:14 pm
Graphicl.fog	55.58	Sun Aug 23 92 12:13 pm

Figure 8.4   View slate

Menu	Dashbord	Samples	Auntjudy.fog
Moose	Fontog35	Fntinstl.wri	Civitype.fog
Nu	Manage	Fontog35.exe	Firi_____.afm
Object	Msapps	Fontog35.hlp	Firi_____.cfg
Reflex	Ontarget	Fontog35.log	Firi_____.inf
Reviews	Painter	Readme.wri	Firi_____.pfb
Savers	System		Firi_____.pfm
Savethis	Temp		Fontinfo.txt
Winbook	Tralblzr		Froman.fog
Windows	_default.pif		Fromita.fog
Winword	256color.bmp		Fromita.fon
Write	Accessor.grp		Fromita.ttf
Www	Antsw.ini		Gcitymod.fog
386spart.par	Applicat.grp		Goudyhun.fog
Autoexec.bat	Apps.hlp		Graphicl.fog

Figure 8.5   List Box view

who keep complicated directory structures on their machines. As is
shown in the following illustration, the user selected the Windows directory in the highest level, which brought up its contents in the second
column. When the user selected a subdirectory there, it brought up a
third column with its contents, and so on (Figure 8.5).

Finally, you can specify an Icon view, much like you'd have on a Mac
(Figure 8.6).

This product has some good-looking icons of its own. Based on the
filename extension, you can remap the icon that represents a file.

Windows inherited DOS' eight-dot-three file naming convention.
While that structure wasn't tragic for a slapdash, thrown-together sec-
ond-generation operating environment such as MS-DOS, it's completely tragic for a new-fangled operating environment such as
Windows. Trailblazer helps rationalize this naming limitation with one
of its most useful features—the ability to add "notes" to any file. Select
a file and press the right mouse button to bring up the Notes window
(Figure 8.7).

You can use free-form text or codify files by subject or index them
with a formal system. If you save the note to the file, it subsequently
appears with a "note attached" symbol next to it (Figure 8.8).

Figure 8.6   Icon view

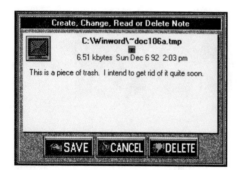

Figure 8.7   The Notes window

There's a straightforward way to get a listing of all Notes with specific text in them, which is described in the later section of this review. This note-making feature is superior to previous generation utilities that search for occurrences of text strings in files, especially for use in Windows. So many of the files you end up searching through are program files or DLLs or little fragments of text or (worst case) the vast multi-megabyte file Windows maintains to manage its Virtual Memory magic that there's an incredible waste of effort. If you can stick with a note-taking routine, Trailblazer's approach is much faster.

As you select directories and files, the slate immediately above the Tree View and View slates keeps track of what you're doing and shows the complete path to your file (Figure 8.9). From this area, the Path slate, you can drag and drop files and folders, but only to and from the On-Deck slate. Jeff and I debated this (and a number of other features) at length. Our conclusion was that someone on the Twisted Pine design team either owned and used an HP calculator or was a devotee of the FORTH programming language. I saw no advantage to the method, only idiosyncrasy.

The arrows at the top right (Figure 8.9) allow you to scroll up and down the path, in case it's so deep you can't see it all. From here, you can double-click on one of the folders higher in the hierarchy, and this folds up the trail that far, displaying that directory's contents in the View slate. Once a file is on the Path slate, you can drag and drop it—*not* to a folder in the Tree View slate or in the View slate, but, as I said, only to the uppermost slate: the On Deck slate.

Figure 8.8   File with "note attached"

Figure 8.9   The Path slate

THE ON DECK SLATE

The On Deck slate is the basic launching pad for commonly used applications and files (Figure 8.10). You can drag a frequently used file or program from the Path slate and drop it into a blank spot on the On Deck slate. Subsequently double-clicking on that icon will launch it. Note, you may have to edit the file extension associations to get documents to run with the proper program. Note also that there's a lot more on this slate than is currently showing; you use the arrows to scroll through offerings here.

The Twisted Pine folk must have known people who worked in a office without a window. The area to the far right of this slate has a time and date clock with a real-time animation of where the sun is in the sky, scrolling the moon at night. Throw in the elegant script, and this is the loveliest clock in the world of Windows utilities.

The On Deck slate, beyond a launching pad for double-clicking on frequently used files, contains icons representing your disk drives. You can drag a file or folder from the Path slate and drop it on the appropriate drive in the On Deck slate. This slate also holds little utilities, or applets, that come with Trailblazer.

 Eraser

Dropping a file or folder on the Eraser erases the subject data exactly like DOS' Delete command.

 Recycle/Delete

Dropping a file or folder on the Recycler icon sets it aside in a holding

Figure 8.10   The On Deck slate

area where you can hold onto it for a specified time or for batch purging, a conservative approach to deleting files.

 Shred/Erase

While Recycler lets you play safe with deletions, the Shredder is the Terminator of erasure. It writes over your file once it's deleted, preventing recovery, which could be useful to people who have sensitive files.

 Run Editor

The Run Editor allows you to launch Windows or DOS applications with command line arguments. You also change icons for the launchable ".RUN" files here. You're going to have to read the manual to make this one work, and even then you'll probably get confused. Just remember two things: Always type the .exe extension to the program you want to run, and retrieve the icon that you create when you Save from the \Trailblazer\Run subdirectory.

 Startup

The Startup utility lets you tag files or applications to launch when Windows starts up. You can also specify its working directory and whether it should run minimized at start-up.

UTILITY SLATE

Adjacent to the Path slate you find the Utility slate (Figure 8.11). It's composed of three small utilities and a button that rolls the Path slate over.

   The three utilities are obvious but useful. The Select All button selects all the files in the current subdirectory. The New button lets you create a new folder (subdirectory) within the current folder (directory). The Help button is your access to an extremely well-executed,

Figure 8.11   The Utility slate

heavily cross-referenced on-line help system. But there are things about this program, such as the necessity of "run files" that are wholly unique and not addressed in the Help. You can find out what to do, but not why, or what it is, exactly, you are doing. Continuing Twisted Pine's UUA design, you *can't* reach their on-line help using the ubiquitous F1 key.

The fourth button, the Command button, forces the Path slate to rotate up and make way, temporarily, for the Command slate.

COMMAND SLATE

Eight Trailblazer buttons comprise the Command slate (Figure 8.12).

The About button

This tells you your system resource availability and has credits (and fake ones, including John Galt) and Twisted Pine's corporate objective.

The Icon button

This takes you to an area where you can assign a wide range of attractive icons to files by filename extension.

The Notes button

This allows you to search for text within notes you've assigned to files. If you press on it, you get the Note-finding window described earlier (Figure 8.13).

Specify the volume you want to search, type in the text string you want to search for, and press the Start button to quickly find all Notes holding the specified text. You can then read all the subject notes, which you can use to better identify files or simply abstract them. You can delete notes from here or "clean" them off a volume. This is a procedure to follow when the file to which the note has been attached is one you've deleted outside of Trailblazer. If you delete files with attached notes within Trailblazer, the product takes care of the note clean-up. The Done button is the UUA equivalent of "Exit."

Figure 8.12 The Trailblazer buttons

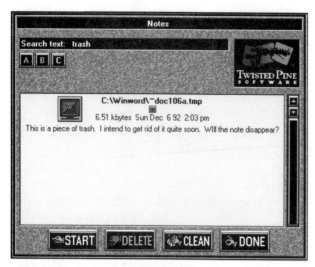

Figure 8.13   Notes window

The Sort button

This lets you specify the order in which files appear in the View Slate: by name, by size, by date, or by extension.

The Find File button

This puts you in an area where you can search for files by name, optionally using wild cards. It's very fast and well presented.

The Launch button

This takes you to a screen where you can add and delete filename extension associations to applications.

The Rename button

This only works if you have a file or group of files selected in the Path Slate. It's a simple DOS rename program. If you're unsure about DOS filename procedures, the manual has an exhaustive explication of it.

The Views button

This lets you specify which of the three described ways Trailblazer shows directory contents in the View Slate.

> Drive C: has **18,055.17** kbytes available and there is **1** item selected totalling [   ] kbytes

Figure 8.14 The Info slate

THE INFO SLATE

There's one last slate, the Info Slate. It's at the bottom of the Trail-blazer screen (Figure 8.14).

It informs you how much disk space is available and how much disk space is occupied by your selection. If your selection is a directory, the little button shown in the preceding image is available; pressing it gives you the size of the selected directory and all its subdirectories.

Product documentation is more than thorough. The manual is beautiful to look at and has better-than-average technical writing. The manual is littered with environmental facts and stimulating questions about the Earth. The on-line help system, as explained earlier, is super, missing perfection only by the omission of graphical clues such as icons and screens. The included tutorial and tutorial files are utilitarian and almost fun.

Summary

We had a real split opinion on this one.

Jeff says: Reading the included materials gives you a strong idea of the people at Twisted Pine. The Benjamin Franklin quotes that hang around for a few seconds when the program boots up tell you much about their work ethic and social views. It's hard to resist calling them up and inviting them over for dinner; they're artistic, interested in the social context of their product, have a strong 101-Ways-to-Save-the-Earth ethic, an explicit interest in end-user feedback, and a commitment to excellence. On the other hand, they've omitted a keyboard shortcut.

Trailblazer is best for people who are comfortable working without much keyboard command action. People who like the spicy individual flavor of this much-better-looking-than-Windows product can really benefit, especially using the Notes feature.

Shops committed to CUA will want to avoid the Twisted Pine offering, as will people, like U.S. Senator Bob Packwood, who believe Northern Spotted owls are best viewed through crosshairs.

Paul says: Using Trailblazer is like encountering someone else's rebellious adolescent child. It's different because it's different, because being different is the goal. There is no higher discernible purpose. It's not easy to learn, it's not faster, it's not better at any significant thing than the native Windows alternatives. It's not worse either, except that you have to learn how to do basic things, like copying files, in a wholly different fashion.

So, if you're a different sort of Windows user or tired of the blandness of CUA applications, this may be what you're looking for to spice up your life. For me it was a rebel without a cause.

9

Direct Access Desktop for Windows 1.0

Overview

Direct Access Desktop for Windows (DAD or DADWIN) is a 43-gallon barrel of features, wrapped around a metaphoric desktop, backup, and virus protection. The fact that version 1.0 is conceptually weird and has bugs from which you can't recover erases the high value contents.

Details

Installation was straightforward. I chose the "Automatic" option, which loads everything and scans your existing drives for Windows applications. This search puts every program, DOS or Windows, on your disk within the organizational capabilities of DAD.

I also chose not to let DAD replace Program Manager as my main Windows shell. I'd advise you to do the same, for starters. Unless DAD wins your heart with its powers and idiosyncrasies, you'll be sad you gave up control.

In each of the desktop managers we review, I've tried to divine what must have been the philosophy, metaphor, or point of view the developer had as his or her point of departure. For DAD I'm convinced it was the Winchester Mystery House—stairways to nowhere, recursive corridors, rooms with no doors...DAD has it all.

THE CONTROL ROOM

Let's begin with the visually busy default main screen, known as the Control Room (Figure 9.1). Note the Asterisk in the upper-left corner. It appears on all windows while you have DAD running. Pressing the asterisk opens up a set of choices for where you want to go from here. I'll explain this further on.

The Drives window is really the front end of the FGS File Manager. Click on a drive icon and FGS File Manager is automatically launched, with a window open on the drive you selected (Figure 9.2).

This is a drag-and-drop File Manager substitute. Its primary distinguishing feature is that some of the most common file operations are implemented as handy buttons across the top. It also allows multiple file selection by simply clicking on additional files—no Alt- or Ctrl- key combinations, as required in the native Windows File Manager.

Offsetting this thoughtful design are some truly boneheaded oversights. Absurdly, if you move, delete, or copy a file, FGS File Manager does not update its windows; consequently, deleted files appear to remain there, and copied files do not appear where you put them. You must take it on faith that the job got done correctly unless and until you force a "refresh" by pressing F5.

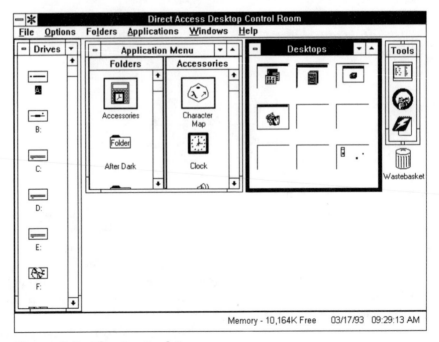

Figure 9.1 The Control Room

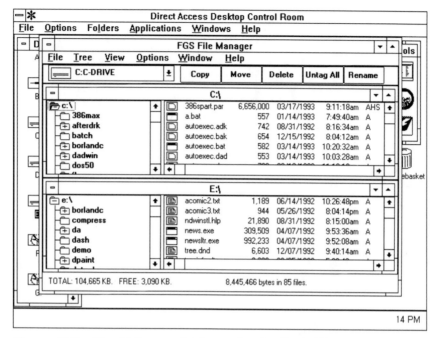

Figure 9.2 The Drives window via the FGS File Manager

This element of design is a throwback to premicrocomputer days, when the dominant (not universal, however) school of program design saw human time as being less expensive than computer time (which it frequently was). With that point of view, you'd never have made the computing engine waste valuable cycles doing something the human "operator" could do. On a time-shared mainframe computer of the 1975 vintage, the cost you'd have to pay to have the system update the screen was prohibitive. And, while this has changed for the better, the world view still lives. There is no technical excuse for having to make the user tell the system to tell itself what's going on so it can tell you without fibbing.

The `Application Menu` contains the program groups on the left. When you double-click on a program group, the group's contents appears on the right (Figure 9.3).

You can launch applications from here, just as you would in Program Manager. Also included here under the `Folders Properties` menu is a warehouse-full of icons for you to use to customize folders and applications. You can also drag these icons to a desktop in the `Desktop` window to launch it there.

Finally, we get to the desktop itself. Like a number of other products, DAD lets you set up different applications or sets of applications in their

Figure 9.3 The Application Menu

own screens, as if each were its own desktop (Figure 9.4). You can rearrange them right here by dragging and dropping them on the desktop
screen. Double-clicking on one takes you to a particular desktop, and
double-clicking on the master asterisk brings you back to the main
area, the Control Room.

If it were that simple all the time, things might not be bad. But DAD
has some unintentional surprises in store for you.

If you launch certain applications like Clock or After Dark, you start
up and cruise along for a bit just fine. But in these cases the applications
just "go away." Or you double-click on a desktop that has nothing running in it. Either way, you end up running against a blank background
with no master asterisk (or anything else) to let you escape or return to
where you were. It is a room with no windows or doors (clue: try double-
clicking in the upper-left corner). If you don't fall for that Dungeons &
Dragons sinkhole, you may be annoyed with the fact that every time you
leave a desktop, the application running in it gets minimized. For example, I typically run Word for Windows full-screen. Having returned

Figure 9.4 Set up your own desktops

to the Control Room to do something else, I come back to Word and find my document suddenly "windowed." DAD helps you out by deciding what mode you want to be in, without consulting you. Also, Jeff experienced frequent freeze-ups (requiring rebooting his system) trying to escape from a desktop to the Control Room.

There's more on my complaint list about the Direct Access Desktop. When you're in it, the task list contains only those applications associated with the desktop you are in, one of which is always Desktop. You can only get to other tasks by first going to their desks, either through the Control Room or directly through the pull-down menu attached to the Master Asterisk. I understand the logic, but choosing Desktop from the task list has no effective meaning, except to deactivate the window you are in—it doesn't actually return you to the Control Room or take you to other desktops or to another application within the current desktop. It doesn't *do* anything, except deactivate the window you are in.

 Wastebasket

The program includes a smart Wastebasket to which you can drag and drop files to dispose of them. It has a timed purge feature that actually gets them off the disk; until that happens or you manually purge, you can retrieve any file you've thrown away, and you don't gain any disk space.

You can open the Wastebasket by double-clicking its icon. The resulting dialog box shows you what files you've put there and offers you the chance to purge them or reclaim them (Figure 9.5).

There are sensible options in the Wastebasket program. You access them from the `Options` menu.

You can specify how much holding space the Wastebasket can have and set the time interval for purging trash (Figure 9.6).

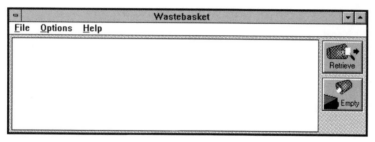

Figure 9.5   A smart Wastebasket

Figure 9.6   Configuring Wastebasket

Fastback Express, a Windows version of Fifth Generation's industry standard floppy disk backup program, is included with DAD. Setup is easy and the program is straightforward, but a note of caution here: If you intend to use this program at its fastest setting, you must test your hardware first. That's to be expected, but, this being Windows rather than DOS, there is a new wrinkle to contend with—multitasking (that is, more than one program executing at a time). The sanity test did not like something I had running in Windows and failed until I removed the offending app. Since the hardware test only runs at installation, the problem arises: What if I do not remember to close that application before trying to do a fast backup? I could be in trouble.

DAD also has a virus detector, Search & Destroy, which is a useful feature, and Power Pad, a beefed-up Notepad/Windows Write compromise that's better than either, but nothing I saw is the world desperate for.

Documentation is problematic, but the poor documentation people need only take about 10 percent of the blame. The package is such a crazy quilt of features, bugs, and eccentric points of view that no one can overcome that. On-line help is a good try, but it fails for the same reason. And if you want to blame the writers, ask yourself this question: Could *you* document the Winchester Mystery House?

Summary

Direct Access Desktop for Windows contains all the right basic features to compete with programs like Norton or Dashboard, but it does not appear to have been completely thought through or tested. The constant irritations in this version 1.0 flaw what might one day become a solid Windows desktop.

10

PC Tools for Windows

Overview

PC Tools for Windows from Central Point Software is a massive under-taking, a cornucopia of code that includes a desktop, an alternative File Manager, and all the other utilities PC Tools users have come to expect in a big utility package.

Details

This program has the best installation program of any software I have ever used. In fact, pieces of PC Tools for Windows are as good as any-thing I've ever seen in terms of design and utilitarian value. But it also contains the most frustratingly incomprehensible and useless software we've seen. Those of you familiar with PC Tools will say, "Hey, that's the way it's always been." Let's look at the good things first and you decide whether it's worth plunking down the money and leaving the foul parts off your system.

Like I said, the installation is a lesson in clarity, and customizing what you want is a breeze.

In the `Custom Setup` you get a complete listing of all the parts and their disk requirements (Figure 10.1). You can pick and choose what you want and see the impact of those choices on your remaining free space. And we are talking *impact*—a full installation clips 14 megabytes off your disk. So, it's worth a little thought about what your needs are.

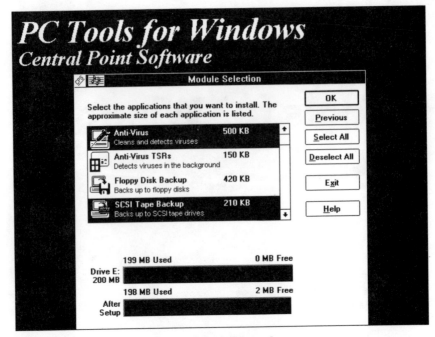

Figure 10.1 Custom setup for PC Tools

One other nice touch in this procedure; Install checks memory for viruses before proceeding, and there's a full anti-virus feature in the package. `Install` also prompts you toward creating a recovery disk, cheap insurance against the inevitable disk crash, or CMOS battery failure.

One thing you *do not* want to do on installation is select the PC Tools Desktop as your default when Windows starts up. Trust me...and for the contrarians, who believe they'll love anything I hate, there is an `Uninstall` feature in the `Setup` program that will let you automatically undo the resulting confusion.

WINSHIELD

Install splits the programs into two groups, WinShield (Figure 10.2) and PC Tools for Windows Desktop. I'll cover WinShield first.

 Undelete

Undelete has come a long way since Peter Norton's first stab at it in DOS eight years ago. PC Tools for Windows version makes the job about as easy and surefire as can be, even on Novell file servers.

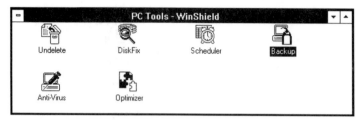

Figure 10.2   WindShield

Figure 10.3 shows a removed directory entry that can be recreated, thanks to the protection feature (called Delete Sentry) that Install put in my AUTOEXEC.BAT. Delete Sentry intercepts any attempt to delete a file and moves it to a hidden directory. This is known among computer vets as a soft delete—the only kind the Mac has ever had. Until the file undergoes a deliberate or scheduled purge, it can be recovered easily, perfectly.

The problem here is that you don't gain any free space in the process, which is often why we delete something to begin with. Two customization features help some—the automatic purge and limit options. These options keep Delete Sentry from growing to hog the disk (Figure 10.4). Now Central Point needs to go the extra mile and offer the option to data compress (a feature their File Manager and Backup programs have) as they hide the file.

You can do without Sentry if you like living dangerously, or you can tell it to only note your deletions. This means the file will be erased but remains recoverable so long as something new recorded to disk does not overwrite the space it occupied.

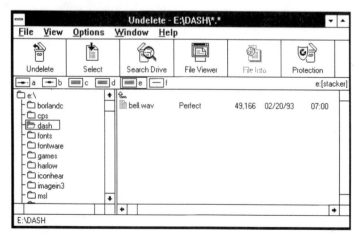

Figure 10.3   Surefire way to undelete files

```
┌──────────────────────────────────────────────────────────┐
│ ─ ╬          Configure Delete Sentry                      │
├──────────────────────────────────────────────────────────┤
│ Which files should Delete Sentry save?        ┌────────┐  │
│ ○ All files                                    │   OK   │  │
│ ● Only specified files:                        └────────┘  │
│                                                ┌────────┐  │
│ Include:              Exclude:                 │ Cancel │  │
│ ┌───────────┬─┐      ┌────────────┬─┐          └────────┘  │
│ │ *.c       │↑│      │ -*.IML     │↑│          ┌────────┐  │
│ │ *.DOC     │ │      │ -*.TMP     │ │          │Drives..│  │
│ │           │ │      │ -*.VM?     │ │          └────────┘  │
│ │           │↓│      │ -*.WOA     │↓│          ┌────────┐  │
│ └───────────┴─┘      └────────────┴─┘          │  Help  │  │
│ Advanced Options                               └────────┘  │
│ ⊠ Do not save archived files                              │
│ Purge files after                                          │
│ ┌─────┐                                                    │
│ │ 7   │ days                                               │
│ └─────┘                                                    │
│ Limit disk space for deleted files to                      │
│ ┌─────┐                                                    │
│ │ 20  │ %                                                  │
│ └─────┘                                                    │
└──────────────────────────────────────────────────────────┘
```

Figure 10.4   Delete Sentry

As suggested by the Undelete main screen, you have comprehensive search features that let you find the file or files you're looking for and even a built-in viewer to verify that you got exactly what you wanted. All in all, this is about as good as it gets in a bad situation.

 Backup

Central Point Backup for Windows has been available for some time, and, while the backup included here appears to have had some features removed, it is a speedy, reliable, and effective way to archive files to floppy disk or a limited number of tape backup units. It couldn't find my Colorado Memories tape drive until research and a few lucky dumb guesses got it aimed in the right direction. Then it forced me to reinstall the program all over again to pick up the floppy backup .DLL (*good thing I like that install program, I see so much of it*).

The first time you use Backup, it analyzes your system. What happened to me illustrates the complexities of doing this sort of system-intensive operation. How PC Tools for Windows handles the situation is instructive. Like all high-speed floppy backups (which try to use direct memory access—DMA) it first runs a safety check, to make sure this engineering cleverness, which originated in Fastback for DOS, will work reliably on your specific machine. PC Tools for Windows detected "lost clusters" on my C: drive and said I would first have to resolve this with either CHKDSK or DiskFix. Now I know that CHKDSK /F declines to run while Windows is present.

DiskFix

So, rather than exit Windows, I decided to give DiskFix a whirl against a *real* problem, those lost clusters.

DiskFix, like Norton Disk Doctor, represents accumulated wisdom about how best and most accurately to recover from most data-loss and file system corruption situations (Figure 10.5). Some of this is under the `Advice` button; the rest is built-in.

While a clever graphical interface entertains you, the Windows version of DiskFix analyzes for all the common forms of file system corruption. DiskFix insisted that I remove almost all my running Windows applications before it would resolve my "lost clusters"—barely one step short of returning to DOS. DiskFix recovered a lost directory and two small chunks of junk. When I deliberately tinkered with a floppy disk and tried the same test, DiskFix accurately recovered a directory and all the files in it. It also made an Undo file on another drive, so the process could be reversed if it didn't work. Note, however, these Undo files can be immense and should be deleted once you are satisfied with the work DiskFix.

All this is not news if you're a DOS émigré, but does suggest that you can now get the same power in Windows that was previously reserved for DOS, with the addition of an informative (and entertaining) graphical interface and context-sensitive help and advice.

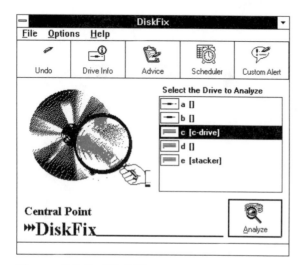

Figure 10.5 DiskFix

Backup (continued)

Now, back to Backup and the integrity test—which ran this time, but failed the high-speed confidence test. Hmm! Remembering the problems I'd had with another product, Fastback for Windows, I removed File Manager and Word for Windows, and of course the high-speed confidence test ran successfully. So, one at a time, I put FileMan and Word back in, and...the confidence test still ran successfully. There was also a serious discrepancy between the total byte count reported by CP Backup and the count from CHKDSK on my Stacker drive. Now, why am I not very confident? It's best, it seems, to make sure all other Windows apps are closed, unless and until experience teaches you otherwise.

Back to my tape drive, I launched a full backup of C: with compression. No surprises. Compression was nearly 50 percent. CP Backup is a mature product, robust, fully configurable, with backup scheduling.

  Scheduler

Scheduler lets you launch applications, such as the Backup or Optimizer, at a predetermined time (Figure 10.6). You first need to aim the Scheduler at a task. The conventional Browse facility lets you find the executable you're interested in, or you can drag and drop documents or applications from either Windows or Central Point's File Manager onto the Scheduler icon.

Now choose the time you want it to run—once, or repeatedly (Figure 10.7).

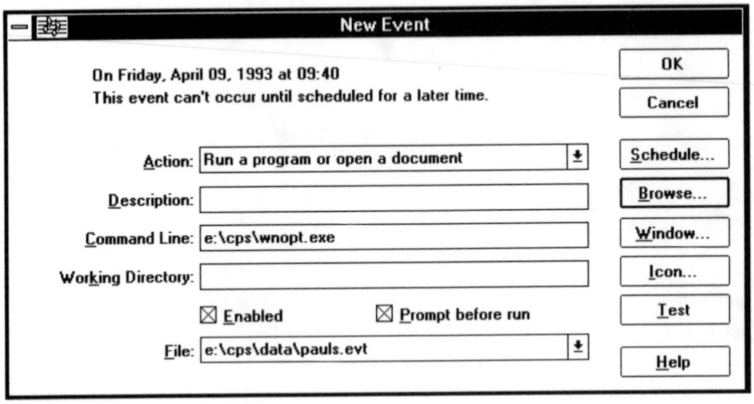

![New Event dialog box. On Friday, April 09, 1993 at 09:40. This event can't occur until scheduled for a later time. Action: Run a program or open a document. Description: (blank). Command Line: e:\cps\wnopt.exe. Working Directory: (blank). Enabled checkbox checked. Prompt before run checkbox checked. File: e:\cps\data\pauls.evt. Buttons: OK, Cancel, Schedule..., Browse..., Window..., Icon..., Test, Help.]

Figure 10.6   Scheduler

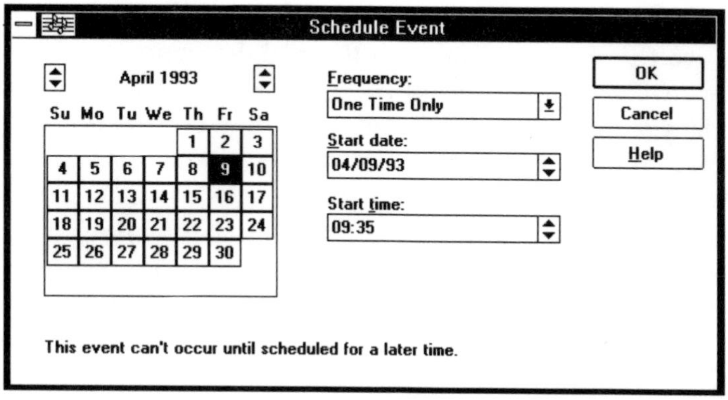

Figure 10.7 Selecting the time to run an application

And you'll see it listed in the main screen (Figure 10.8).

Now you minimize the Scheduler and it waits to do the assigned work. Remember to place Scheduler in your Startup Group. It must be running with a specified event file to run the tasks assigned. Note also that complicated network, or backup, or modem tasks can run into other conflicts. Think this process through. And test, test, test before you trust.

 Anti-Virus

This is the safe-computing element of the WinShield group. I once argued with a leading publisher that anti-virus programs were a fad. I

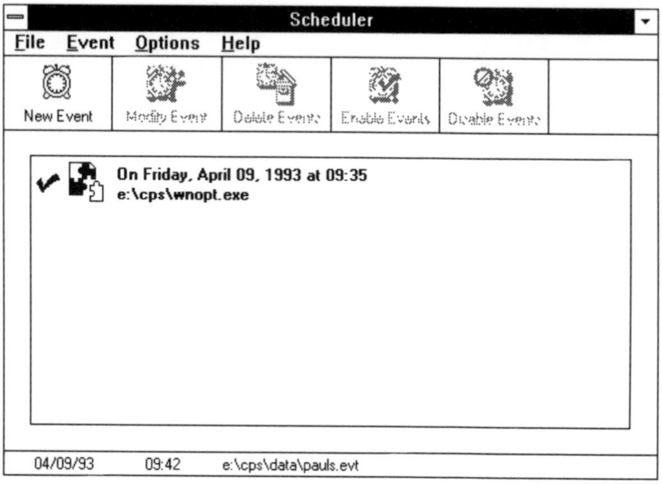

Figure 10.8 Scheduler listing

woke up the next morning and called him back to argue the opposite, that I was wrong, and that human nature and the nature of computing being inescapably what they are, this would always be a small but serious, real, daily concern. Computer viruses—that is, programs designed to scare you into thinking your data have been destroyed or actually to wipe out valuable work—do exist and anyone can be stricken. While the best defense is a good backup, running an anti-virus program such as this one is a sane and simple precaution.

Installation executes the anti-virus program first and gives you the option of making it a part of your power-up routine (Figure 10.9). You can also run CP Anti-Virus as you wish.

How viruses work, how you detect them, and what to do about it are beyond the scope of this volume. Central Point documents the subject well—and all you really need to do to get most benefits is run the program.

But lest you doubt the scope of the problem, a listing of viruses and virus-like programs is included (Figure 10.10). Note the total. This is just the list CP Anti-Virus dealt with at release time; trust that the number of viruses has grown since, and you'll need to update CP Anti-Virus in the future.

 Optimizer

Last piece of the WinShield group is Central Point's disk Optimizer, a disk and file defragmenter. Again, this is a mature product, and that's

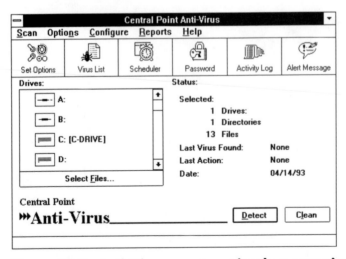

Figure 10.9 Anti-Virus: a sane, simple precaution

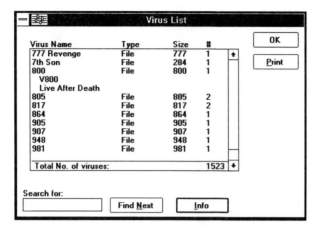

Figure 10.10 Listing of viruses in Anti-Virus

what you want in a defragger. Still, it is wise to make a current backup before running any optimizing software, until you are confident that it works perfectly on your system every time.

Optimizer refused to run when I tested it. It said VOPTD.386 was missing. There was no documentation for this (or any other) error message in either the paper manual or on-line help. So I revisited Install (still painless, but, by this point, getting boring) and it fixed things by adding a "device" statement under [386Enh] for the missing driver. It's this sort of thing that belies all the hype about Windows being a relief from the complexities of DOS (Mac System 7.x is no dolt's paradise either). That is, unless you think it's reasonable and simple that when a light bulb burns out, you should rebuild your house from the foundation up. It's either that or learn to screw with the details, which is why DOS (and UNIX) lovers feel their system is more honest: They have no illusions of "ease of use."

Pick a drive and Optimizer gives you a map (Figure 10.11). Since each little block can represent many clusters of data (57 in the case of my drive C:, or 116,736 bytes), the map is only a crude approximation. Want to know what files are depicted by a certain block? Double-click, wait for a calculation, and you get a listing.

Figure 10.12 has the two files at the end of my C: drive. They happen to be hidden system files used for data recovery. Compress (and all other defraggers worth trusting) won't move them.

Now, depending how compulsively neat and orderly you are, you might want your files physically arranged on the disk just so. Optimize supports your desire with several options (Figure 10.13).

Practically speaking, order has almost no noticeable effect on performance for most systems. Optimizing free space has the most effect

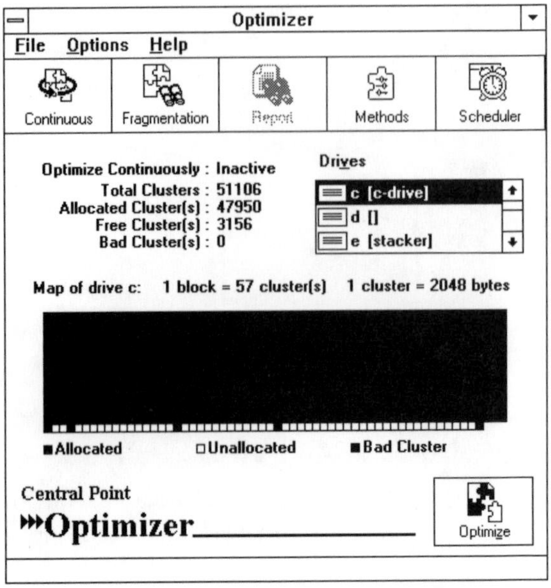

Figure 10.11 Optimizer

on reducing future fragmentation, but Windows and DOS combine to undo you over the course of a day, so the benefits are fleeting. Note, however, the "Clear" options. Know that defragging your disk overwrites data, making recovery of lost and deleted information impossible. You can reduce this to "near impossible" by choosing the "Do Not Clear" option.

Know also that some people, both in and out of government, desire old information to be destroyed. For most of us, once is enough, and "Quick Clear" will overwrite all the free space with nonsense. But the National Security Agency knows that they, at least, can read data that has been overwritten six times; hence, the DOD standard erase overwrites seven times. (Rumor had it that two years ago the NSA, ever more resourceful, was up to reading data erased eight times. I call this the Nixon standard.)

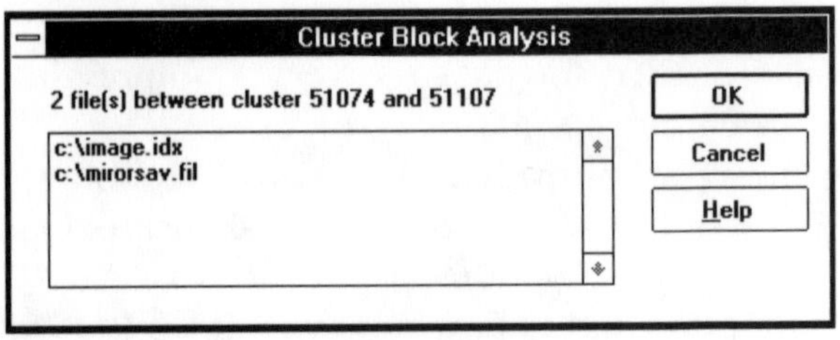

Figure 10.12 Block locations

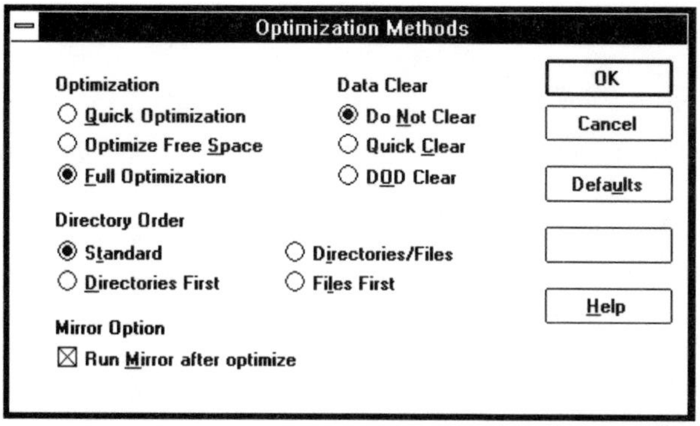

```
┌─────────────────────────────────────────────────────┐
│ ─              Optimization Methods                   │
├─────────────────────────────────────────────────────┤
│                                         ┌──────────┐  │
│  Optimization          Data Clear       │    OK    │  │
│  ○ Quick Optimization  ◉ Do Not Clear   └──────────┘  │
│  ○ Optimize Free Space ○ Quick Clear    ┌──────────┐  │
│  ◉ Full Optimization   ○ DOD Clear      │  Cancel  │  │
│                                         └──────────┘  │
│  Directory Order                        ┌──────────┐  │
│  ◉ Standard          ○ Directories/Files│ Defaults │  │
│  ○ Directories First ○ Files First      └──────────┘  │
│                                         ┌──────────┐  │
│                                         │          │  │
│  Mirror Option                          └──────────┘  │
│  ☒ Run Mirror after optimize            ┌──────────┐  │
│                                         │   Help   │  │
│                                         └──────────┘  │
└─────────────────────────────────────────────────────┘
```

Figure 10.13   Custom configuration of Optimization

Ready to optimize? Not so fast. If you plan on running any Windows applications that do file access, forget it. They'll stop Optimizer (safely) in its tracks.

Now! You can watch the colored blocks blink mysteriously, or go have coffee. One hundred not-very-fragmented megabytes took about 15 minutes to organize.

So the news here is that, once again, what you had in DOS you now have under Windows, without extra benefits, but without having to bring Windows down and revert to the cursed DOS cursor.

PC TOOLS FOR WINDOWS DESKTOP

Okay, I've been avoiding it, but here we are, at what should be the centerpiece of the package. I've been living with Desktop for a month now, I've read the documentation, and I still don't understand it.

You'll recall (or soon encounter) the idea with desktop organizers that each of them has some central organizing principle or metaphor or strategy (rooms, dashboard, squeegee, desk) to which it is, at least nominally, faithful. Central Point says there are *offices* with *desktops* that have *items* on them either separately or in *folders*. Ja, sure, nothing challenging here, I figured. Not!

Figure 10.14 is a typical opening screen. The major piece of real estate here is Program groups, which are your Program Manager groups stuffed into file folders. You'll notice there is also a folder labeled Program group. This, it turns out, is the same as the Windows Program group. Double-clicking on it merely makes the associated Window active—the folder does not go away; it is what is known in the programming trade as "modal." How it behaves depends on something else—in this case, that it has already been clicked on, so it can't really *do* anything.

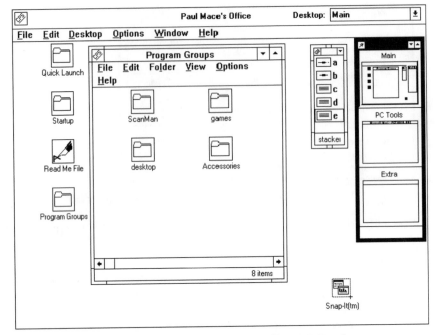

Figure 10.14   Typical opening screen for PC Tools

The problem with modal objects is that the user must learn by experience what will happen under certain circumstances and commit that knowledge to memory. I confess I suffer from modal intolerance and instantly dislike designs which force me to learn things that serve no apparent purpose except that the programmers wrote it that way.

Also on this screen we have:

- A drive toolbar, which not only lists the available drives, but serves as a quick launch for the PCTW File Manager.

- Quick menus accessible by pointing at things and clicking the right mouse button.

- A desktop thumbnail, or bird's eye view, called Multi-Desk, which shows all your desktops and some colored areas representing what is lying on them. Moving the cursor over the colored squares causes a label to appear showing you what it is you're pointing at. You can go to a desktop by double-clicking here, pulling down the desktop category at the top-right of the screen, or clicking on the master control icon in the upper left and choosing the switch-to menu option. Note that task switching via the Alt-Tab key combination *is limited to the items on the desktop you are in.* And switching to the "desktop" task, which would be "Main" in the case of the Main desktop, can be confusing if you have something like, say, Word for Windows open full-screen, as this merely causes the PCTW title bar to appear—another extra meaningless choice you learn to avoid. Confused? Read on.

The problem here is this "Main" desktop is not drag-and-drop. That means, contrary to what the documentation implies, you cannot move things around at this level by grabbing their file folders and icons—that ol' modality thing again. (You *can* move the little colored squares from one desktop to another in the thumbnail view, however.)

Also, I couldn't find any way to add a new desktop or rename an old one. Oh, the menu options were on the dialog boxes, but they were always grayed out. I tried to do it as documented—no luck. I stopped. Life is too short. There is a lot to like about PC Tools for Windows, but the Desktop is not, in this release, one of them.

 Format

With marvelous concision of purpose, this does what it says.

 Synchronize Directory

This is a neat tool, especially for networkers. It lets you automatically copy files between directories (or whole branches) on the same or different drive's letters, thus duplicating or "reconciling" the two.

 Copy

Copies one floppy disk to another.

 File Manager

Philosophically, this is Windows' File Manager with *major* refinements. Expanding the directory tree can be controlled by level buttons—a feature lifted from X-Tree. And the right mouse button gets you a quick menu that includes both encryption (for the security conscious) and compression (for the rest of us). That means you can Zip or Arc files with the File Manager, the better alternative to blowing them away when disk space gets precious. This feature alone is compelling enough to switch to PCTW File Manager.

But, remember, all you Stacker and DoubleSpace mavens: Files on these drives are already LZW compressed. *Compressing them again actually expands them*—trust me. You are going backwards and wasting time in the process.

Worthwhile in this same vein is the ability to view an entire drive's files, regardless of sub-directory structure, as a single, flat list, sorted by size or name or such. This is, in some ways, an easier way to search than using a search utility. And you can effectively delete the largest files you no longer need when searching for precious disk space.

PCTW File Manager includes a smart file viewer, so you can peek at documents and data directly, with all the popular file formats translated to make sense.

In short, PCTW File Manager is one of the things Central Point got absolutely dead-on.

File Viewer

File Viewer, which is also available from within File Manager, lets you peek at files quickly, with most popular formats translated so you actually see them represented as they would be within, says, Word Perfect or Excel. It is also available through the File Manager.

SmartFind

SmartFind is a file locator utility. It allows you to specify all sorts of filters to find only the files you want—a certain size, certain dates, certain directories on certain drives.

In Figure 10.15, I looked on my C: and E: drives for any documents that referenced Central Point. This utility is more powerful than what's available under the File Manager, but it's probably overkill unless you're on a network or searching a gigabyte-sized disk.

Script Tools

This is PCTW's macro recorder. It leads us into a product area that is beyond the scope of this book—Windows macro languages. A recorder actually writes out a description of what Windows is doing, then reinterprets what it writes to play it back with:

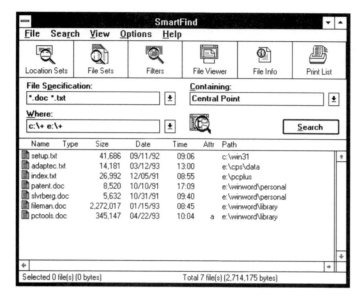

Figure 10.15   Finding Central Point files via SmartFind

 Script Runner

This is the companion piece to the recorder. You can, if you wish, edit a script manually, or write one from scratch in the macro language. This requires sophistication neither Jeff nor I wholly possess, nor wish to.

 System Consultant

Here's a quick set of diagnostics, similar in some respects to those in WinMaster and QA+ (Figure 10.16).

I picked the *Windows Summary* screen because all of the topics on the right are "hot"—click on them and you get as deep a look as anyone could want at Windows innards.

Figure 10.17 is a look at Windows resources, which are what you run out of long before memory or disk space are exhausted. Until Windows NT came along, you were limited to 64K each of system resources and GDI (Graphics Display Interface) objects. Anything that is actually running in memory taxes these resources, meaning Windows itself (which is not one program, but many, like some aquatic colony organism) and your default shell (Progman). Here you get some idea of which applications are soaking up what precious space—my Tek Phaser color Postscript printer driver, for instance.

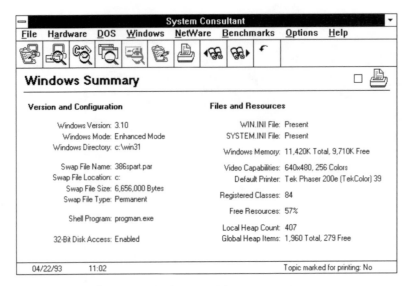

Figure 10.16   System diagnostics

In fact, the level of detail is greater than any other package we re-viewed—so much so that some context-sensitive help would be useful.

One place you can go for real, useful help is the `System Recommendations` (Figure 10.18). Here is good, simple wisdom about how to improve performance without spending much time or any money.

Jeff is *InfoWorld*'s reviewer for diagnostic utilities and has seen most of them. He believes this has one of the cleanest and most useful de-signs around. And he agrees with me that System Consultant, on the whole, is another one of the things Central Point got right-on.

Windows Resources

Address	Handle	Size	Owner	Resource Type
8092:EC80	0x26EE	1,152	PHASER	User Defined
8092:F400	0x02EE	288	DISPLAY	Cursor Component
8095:30E0	0x0876	1,120	PHASER	User Defined
8078:2C40	0x0996	4,352	PHASER	User Defined
8097:5840	0x220E	1,536	MMSYSTEM	RCDATA
8090:3820	0x025E	32	DISPLAY	Cursor
8090:3840	0x07E6	1,184	DISPLAY	Icon Component
8090:9220	0x02E6	288	DISPLAY	Cursor Component
8090:A040	0x159E	1,184	PROGMAN	Icon Component
8090:AC40	0x0306	288	DISPLAY	Cursor Component

☒ Accelerators ☒ Dialogs ☒ Icons ☒ RCDATA
☒ Bitmaps ☒ Error Tables ☒ Menus ☒ Strings
☒ Cursors ☒ Fonts ☒ Name Tables ☒ User Defined

Figure 10.17   Clicking on a topic in the Windows Summary screen

System Recommendations

Reduce the value of the BUFFERS setting to improve cache performance
Increase the value of DMABufferSize in your SYSTEM.INI file

The disk-caching program you are using will perform better if you reduce the "BUFFERS=30" setting in your CONFIG.SYS file to "BUFFERS=10". However, you should not make this change if an application in your system requires the higher value.

Figure 10.18   Advice on improving system performance

 Icon Editor

The Icon Editor is a minor utility, brilliantly rendered here. It comes with a storehouse of pre-made icons you can use as is or re-edit. Many of these icons are for specific applications such as Ami or Excel or DOS. You can import other icons for editing and add them to the libraries provided.

The utility has as simple and elegant an interface as is possible to render (Figure 10.19).

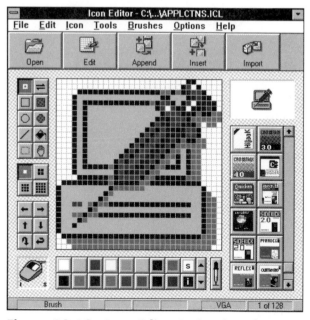

Figure 10.19   Icon Editor's simple, elegant interface

Summary

For the aggregate contained in the box known as PC Tools for Windows, I would say, "It is the best of class, it is the worst of class." Elements such as the File Manager, System Consultant, and Install programs make this offering a Ruthian accomplishment. The Backup and Optimizer are stalwart. But the rest of the work here has blemishes and bugs and left bitter experiences that make me cautious about recommending them to anyone who's impatient or not excited about learning new, undocumented paradigms.

11

Conclusions

So, after a year of entertaining available alternatives to Windows as it is shipped, where am I at?

Program Manager Alternatives

Figure 11.1 is what my opening screen looks like now.

Not Norton, not Dashboard, not Rooms for Windows, but Program Manager—yup, that's what you see there at the bottom. So what happened, other than I changed background pictures?

I never did cotton to Norton the way Jeff did. Having no history of Mac zealotry, it appeared Norton was just, well...different to be different. Rooms intrigued me, but was ponderous and not fully thought out. Dashboard was a lot of fun, and didn't much get in the way, but I honestly don't sit at the computer for fun much—you won't find me taking a quick, refreshing 30 minutes to shoot Nazis in Castle Wolfenstein. I'm here to work, or I'm gone. And none of these, or the other Program Manager substitutes I looked at, improved my work environment to any measurable degree; they merely substituted one kind of organizing principle for another.

Working my way through these alternative Windows lifestyles reminds me very much of what I've experienced at my own company and witnessed in other organizations, an incessant drive to re-engineer the way things are managed. As a human compulsion, it is akin to

Figure 11.1   Paul's opening screen

rearranging the furniture and spring cleaning, this recurring urge toward greater order—or any order at all, so long as it is not our own. We
cannot shake a fundamental belief in some ideal pattern that resists
decay while our backs are turned, resists our own efforts, both willful
and unwitting, to leave chaos in our wake.

Choosing a desktop manager is the same as choosing a Zen master
or a church or a management guru; you are choosing a discipline, an
objectified way of doing things, rules and regulations to which you must
submit in order to be saved from yourself.

In the end I suppose I didn't find Master Norton any more enlight-
ened than Master Xerox or Master Gates. I found what I have found in
life in general, that I must master myself to the greatest extent possible
and accept that this mastery will be permanently evolving and always
incomplete. No computer program, GUI or otherwise, is going to
change who I am or how I behave. At best, I pray, it will let me behave
like myself, with whom I am at uneasy peace. And, thus, the iconized
Progman—I want what I've always wanted in an interface, for it to get
the hell out of my way.

So, What Do I Want?

If I could steal bits and pieces of the programs I looked at and create my own alternatives, that would be something!

There's no real reason technically why you couldn't do that. One of the promises of Windows, and Bill Gates' vision of how it should work, is that there are no major applications, just a big bag of software parts that can be assembled to do different things for different people.

It's called OLE 2.0 and it's not here yet. It may never get here at the level of granularity I'm asking for. But it is just possible, one day, I'll be able to build my own electronic desktop, or flight deck, by dragging and dropping the best features from 40-some alternatives, costing an aggregate kilobuck, and be, well . . . not happy, but at ease.

More likely I am doomed to Alt-Tab-Right-click-F1 my way through life on the electronic desktop until programmers and program designers get it through their skulls that I am not looking to them for philosophy or salvation but for a variety of tools to save myself time and work.

I have often argued that computers should come to us with the cultural attainments of a good high school graduate. People invariably shudder. But the computer already comes to you with a bias, that of the priestly caste of engineers and designers who make the software and hardware you must live with. Have you met these people? I live and work with them—heaven help me, I am one! So is Bill Gates and Peter Norton and all the wonderful, uncelebrated young women and men who are inventing and expanding this electronic universe every day. If you're looking to people like us and the things we make to make you happy, you should seek counseling soon.

What About Jeff?

When we were all done he went out and bought a new Mac.

SECTION 3

Documentation

12

Tools

Six utilities are contained on the disk that is included with this book:

- NoFrag—disk reorganizer and file defragmenter
- MapDrive—disk file mapper, that shows fragmentation
- DosGate—mouse right-click escape to DOS
- TmpErase—a quick way to list and erase temporary files
- FileFind—a file locating tool
- FileSpy—a file activity tracker from Software Workshop Inc.

Installation

Place the distribution diskette in a drive—for example, A:—and choose File|Run A:\SETUP.EXE in the Windows Program Manager. Or, from the File Manager, select the drive you placed the diskette in and double-click on SETUP.EXE. This program will install all six utilities in a directory called MTOOLS on your C: drive. If you prefer, you may select a drive other than C: or create a different directory during the installation process—a dialog box will appear to prompt you. The installation program also creates a program group called "Tools for Windows" in Windows' Program Manager that contains an icon for each of the six utilities. To use NoFrag, MapDrive, DosGate, TmpErase, or FileFind, just double-click on the appropriate icon.

Before you can use FileSpy, however, you must also place the following line in your CONFIG.SYS file:

```
DEVICE=C:\MTOOLS\HISPY.SYS
```

If you selected a different drive and/or a different directory during the installation for the utilities, use the new drive and/r directory in place of `C:\MTOOLS` in `CONFIG.SYS`.

You can use the Windows SYSEDIT program to insert the above line in your `CONFIG.SYS` file. SYSEDIT is not automatically installed when you put Windows on your machine, so you may have to install it yourself by using the Program Manager `File|New|Program` feature. Browse in the `WINDOWS/SYSTEM` directory for `SYSEDIT.EXE`. You may also use the Notepad program in Windows (it should be in your Accessories program group) to edit your `CONFIG.SYS` file. Remember, it is always a good idea to make a copy of your `CONFIG.SYS` before you make changes to it.

You will have to reboot your computer before you can use FileSpy.

NoFrag

A hard disk–reorganizing and file-defragmenting utility, NoFrag is designed to accomplish the two most important things a defragger can do: Keep free disk space consolidated into a single block and keep data files in as few pieces as possible, preferably one piece.

WHAT IS FRAGMENTATION?

And why should you care, you might also ask. I'll try to explain.

Disks are usually just that, a circular storage medium made up of one or more platters, floppy or hard, and read-write heads that scan a magnetic coating on the disk's top and bottom surfaces, laying down and picking up a data recording signal. Disks are physically divided up into concentric recording rings, called tracks. These tracks are further divided, like a pie, into segments called sectors. This lets the computer break up the recording into little chunks.

Because no one (who had any influence) ever imagined the capacity of our disks (or Bill Gates' net worth) would be measured in billions, the DOS file system was born incapable of handling more than 32 kilo-chunks of data (raised to 65,535 chunks in DOS 3.0). Fortunately, there was such a disparity between the 160K floppy and then common 5-megabyte hard disks that another, adjustable layer of indirection was added to DOS to clump adjacent disk sectors together. Chunks made up of one or more segments, or sectors, became known as clusters. As a consequence, DOS can be made to deal with disks of almost unlimited capacity by bumping up this "cluster size," so long as the total cluster count remains under 65535.

Physical cluster size is determined when the disk is partitioned and formatted, and as a rule you have no say in it. Each cluster represents a specific number of adjacent sectors on the physical disk and often exceeds 32,736 bytes per cluster on large disks.

We're going to skip over one aspect of inefficiency here: Even a file containing but a single character will get a whole cluster of disk space—the larger the disk capacity, the more space wasted by small files. Instead, we'll look at the bright side: As files grow, they can potentially relinquish and reacquire clusters, so they only take up space they really need.

Mostly, of course, files grow, which is a corollary to Parkinson's law: Data will grow to fill all storage space available. Knowing this, all computer disk operating systems (that's what DOS stands for) employ schemes for squeezing new data randomly into space available, wherever that may be.

In PC- and MS-DOS, the scheme is called the FAT system, for file allocation table. The FAT is simply a linear listing of all the clusters on a disk. When you add enough data to a file so that it requires a whole new cluster of disk space—say, one more character to a 512-byte file—DOS searches the FAT for a free cluster. If the file was originally given FAT entry 2, and entry 3 is free, then all is well, and the file merely gets recorded in the next adjacent physical space. But something else may—and almost certainly will—have occupied cluster 3 in the course of your daily computing. No problem; DOS finds cluster 3000 is free and gives your file that space instead. In the future (which may be only 3 milliseconds away) when an application sends DOS looking for data, DOS looks in the directory entry for this file, learns that it starts in cluster 2, then checks the FAT to see that what was begun in 2 is now continued in 3000. The file is intact, but physically segmented. So what's the problem?

Remember those recording tracks a few paragraphs back? Cluster 2 and cluster 3000 are separated by a lot of data. For certain, the two clusters are not recorded on the same physical track. That means the read/write heads must move from one place to another on the disk. This is accomplished by little electromechanical devices that move the heads in very small, precise steps, to and from the edge of the disk. These "steppers" can position the heads dead-center over a very fine recording track—much less than the width of a human hair. As wonderful and wizardly as these devices are, they are the *slowest* component associated with your computer—except for you.

Now, imagine your file has continued to grow, as you add names, addresses, customer records, orders, and inventory, day after day. Cluster after cluster is concatenated to the file, and DOS doesn't care one whit about keeping the chain physically straight. Nor does it know that you are about to expand the file several clusters of data at once. It just looks for the next single free cluster beyond where it last found one. Thus, what is, on the one hand, a virtue—the ability to add or subtract any free cluster of storage randomly to or from any file, on demand—leads to the random physical placement of what is logically a single, continuous sequence of information. And this makes for the sometimes vicious and time-consuming ratchet of read/write heads back and forth in search of the next link of data in a file.

This can bring programs that are data-intensive to their knees, and you to tears, because your business is irretrievably computerized. Suddenly, all the promised efficiencies of computerization appear to have evaporated. Faster computers and bigger disks make no difference, because the problem is inherent in all disk operating systems, especially in PC/MS-DOS and the FAT system.

WHAT'S THE SOLUTION?

Windows NT and OS/2 promise a high-performance files system that will alleviate the problem. While they are better at postponing fragmentation, they have their own inherent problems, paramount of which is that they are incompatible with the FAT system. So you're going to have to choose, which means you get to experience another "transition" in technologies, as well as the fear, uncertainty, and doubt that is associated with it. (Make backups.)

Right now a disk cache such as PC-Kwik or Speedcache+ will help, by keeping frequently accessed data in fast RAM. But the best solution is for some program to rearrange the segments of data intelligently in linear, physical sequence—and all the free space on the disk in one, big, solid chunk. Some additional performance improvement can be obtained by rearranging files into specific sequences and defragmenting subdirectories, which are stored just like files. But the biggest performance bonus by far comes from simply defragmenting the disk and consolidating free space.

There are commercial defraggers, such as Central Point's Optimizer, and they all have their virtues and vices. These defraggers generally take a while to run, often several hours, and they require the full use of your PC. So while they are running, you can't play games, use your word processor, or what have you. But NoFrag works only while your PC is idle, permitting you to use your PC when you need to, and activating as soon as you're finished.

Think of NoFrag as a tireless but timid robot. Whenever you touch the mouse or the keyboard, it will stop and hide. After a delay (controlled by you) it will go back to work. It is not afraid of other programs, and works right alongside them. It works on all versions of DOS greater than 3.0, and it loves disk caches and Stacker and Double Space drives—in fact it works on anything that appears as a local drive to Windows, no matter what the true nature or capacity of the drive. And it does so with pull-the-plug safety. It will also work while your screen-saver program is active.

NoFrag first attempts to consolidate all free space in a single block at the inside of the disk—the bottom of the map. It then begins defragging in earnest. When it's done as much as it can, it reconsolidates the drive. This process continues until NoFrag can no longer improve things; it then moves on to the next drive.

The default for NoFrag is to run as an icon and to indicate in the icon label which drive it is defragmenting (Figure 12.1). You'll see mapping activity inside the icon as it runs, but that's the only indication you'll have that something's happening. The real activity is occurring behind the scenes.

To change parameters, left-click on the icon and select Control Box (Figure 12.2). This brings up the Control Panel, which allows you to adjust the delay in activating NoFrag (Delay), to switch between using an icon and a full screen to chart NoFrag's progress (FullScrn), and to select the drives that you wish to have defragged (Drives). When you are finished making changes to the parameters, just close the Control Panel.

Delay is the number of minutes NoFrag will wait, after any mouse or keyboard activity, before resuming defragging. One minute is the least amount of time you can select; 9999 minutes is the most. You'll probably want to have a delay of between one to five minutes to get the most out of NoFrag.

FullScrn is a checkbox that indicates you want NoFrag to run as a full-screen map, rather than as an icon (Figure 12.3). To save time,

Figure 12.1   NoFrag as a minimized, but active icon

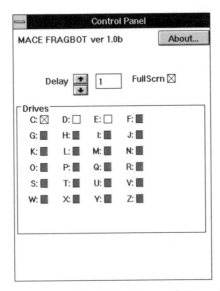

**Figure 12.2   Use Control Panel to
set NoFrag parameters**

NoFrag *does not* map the current status of the drive, except to locate all open space. If you want to see where files are located, you'll have to run

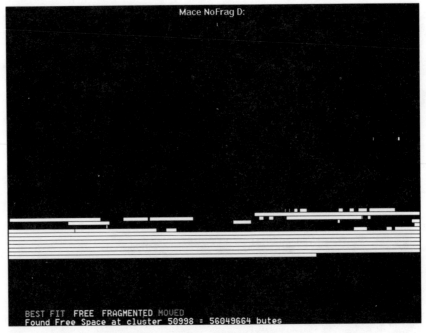

Figure 12.3   NoFrag as full-screen map

MapDrive. NoFrag does map the open space on your drive, both in its icon and full-screen forms, as it goes, so you have some idea of the activity taking place.

Unlike drive maps in other defraggers, this is not an approximation. Each little vertical line represents one cluster of storage. Depending upon the capacity of your drive, the lines may be taller or shorter, but they still represent whole clusters.

As files are moved you will see the colors in the NoFrag may change to reflect activity. Cyan marks *BEST FIT*, files that are candidates to be moved when closing empty spaces. White represents *FREE* space, which will be filled and consolidated. Dark blue represents *OCCUPIED* areas that have not yet been mapped or moved—some of which may be open files or protected files such as Windows' swapfile, which can never be moved. Green represents files that have been *MOVED*. Yellow files are *FRAGMENTED* files that will be moved and made into one piece.

Drives are the checkboxes that select on which drives NoFrag will work. When it can no longer improve the first drive selected, NoFrag moves to the next. Once it's finished the list, it returns to the first and begins again. If a drive letter shows as a gray box, that drive is not eligible—probably because it is a network drive, tape, or CD-ROM. NoFrag will continue to run until you stop it.

That's all there is to it. This version does not defragment directories, nor allow you neatness buffs to specify file order. For all but a few of you it will achieve 90 percent of the performance improvement you could expect from other commercial defraggers.

When you are satisfied you understand and like what NoFrag does, you might want to copy it to the Startup group.

MapDrive

The drive mapper shows an accurate representation of the way space is allocated on the selected drive, similar to NoFrag's full-screen mapper, only more complete. MapDrive is an exact map of the FAT, with one small, colored, vertical stripe for each cluster on the drive. Here is your chance to see illustrated what I talked about in the NoFrag section— how DOS mangles the allocation of space on your drive.

Since DOS 3.0, the following logic has been in use: When you start the computer, or reboot with `Ctrl-Alt-Del`, DOS resets an internal pointer to cluster 2, which is the first available storage spot on the disk. The next time a request is received to add a free cluster to an existing file or create a new file, DOS counts up from 2 until it finds an empty cluster and writes the data there. It then resets the pointer to indicate the last spot written. Even if files are deleted and free spots are opened in the FAT below the current pointer, DOS continues to count up, until it reaches the end of the FAT (or you reboot), at which point it begins counting at 2 again.

As you can see, this is a fairly dumb way of doing things. One of the results is that programs such as database sorts—which often work by writing a new, sorted file, deleting the original, and renaming the new file to the old filename—effectively unpack the disk. Big holes open up magically in the map, and files seem to hop into what was free space. This is the result of the DOS logic at work. The minute you've finished optimizing and defragging and gone back to work, DOS starts conspiring to undo what you've accomplished.

Also, note the big blue block of occupied space on your map of C: or D:. That is Windows' swapfile, which you should make permanent. It cannot and will not move. DOS and NoFrag and other defraggers and optimizers must work around it. So, on the drive that has your Windows swapfile, free space can rarely be consolidated into a single block—not until you've filled the disk beyond the position of the swapfile.

When you launch it, MapDrive gives you the opportunity to select the drive you want (Figure 12.4). Make a selection and close that dialog box, and the mapping begins.

OPEN files continue to show in dark blue, while areas *USED* by unopened files are mapped in cyan. *SYSTEM* files are marked in red, and *FRAGMENTED* files in yellow. If you move the mouse or strike a key, the map will be erased and redrawn. To exit, double-click on the master control button in the upper-left corner.

DosGate

This is the simplest of the utilities, and the one some of you will use the most. Launch it, and from there you can escape to DOS by double-clicking on any title bar, active or not. Type EXIT at the DOS prompt to return to Windows. You may also want to include this utility in your Startup group.

Note: If you have another application running that makes use of the right mouse button double-click, this will not work. This version does not allow you to re-assign a different mouse-key combination.

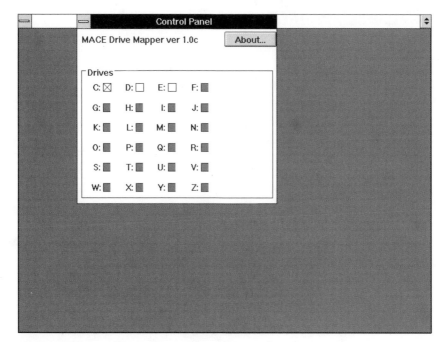

Figure 12.4 MapDrive Control Panel

TmpErase

Windows applications are forever stranding temporary files (extension .TMP) on your disk and wasting megabytes of space. This tool makes getting rid of them simple.

When you launch it, TmpErase searches the default drive (C:) and lists all the .TMP files (Figure 12.5). You may then select one for erasure or delete them all. You may also select additional drives to be searched.

Note: TmpErase will not erase the open files Windows is currently using—denoted with a +.

FileFind

Another single-purpose tool, FileFind finds the file you indicate on the drive(s) you select. Fill in the name or use wild card characters, select a drive or drives to search, and click on Search with the mouse (Figure 12.6).

FileFind offers the added advantage of showing which files are fragmented. Check the FragChk box and you'll see fragmented files

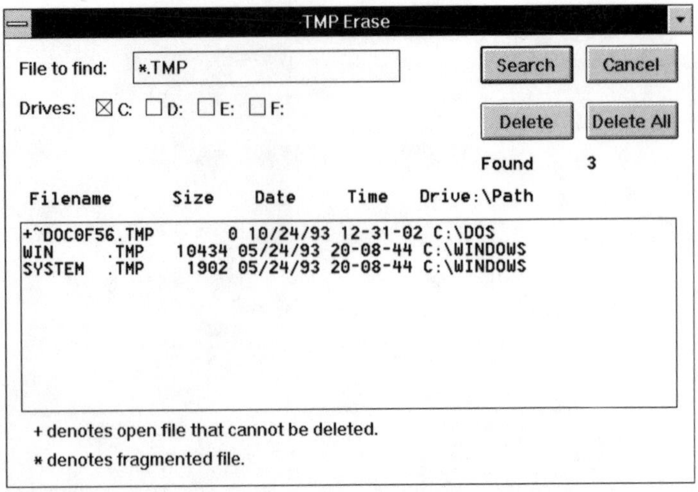

Figure 12.5   TmpErase removes temporary files

marked with an asterisk *. Note, this can take several minutes if you search for *.* (that is, every file on the disk).

FileSpy

FileSpy is an introductory version of Software Workshop Incorporated's Hard Impact. FileSpy tracks all file activity on your computer. It displays which files are being opened in Windows and DOS. It also makes a list of Windows activity.

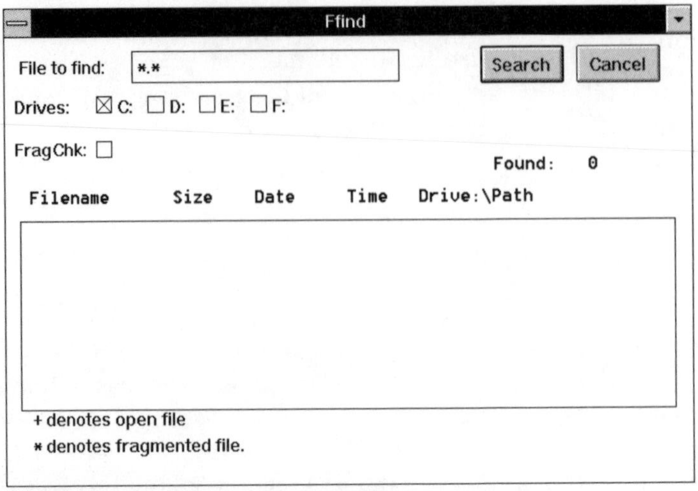

Figure 12.6   FileFind finds files

Here's your chance to see why Windows is such a Bowser, especially if you don't use a disk cache or fail to set the Windows Swapfile optimally. Most of you probably believe the only file you have open is the one you are working on in your word processor, spreadsheet, or database. That was true in DOS, but be prepared to be amazed: In Windows *everything* is a file—programs, data, fonts, colors, printers. Files are Windows' fleas, and, as Jonathan Swift foretold:

> So, naturalists observe, a flea
> Hath smaller fleas that on him prey;
> And these have smaller fleas to bite 'em,
> And so proceed *ad infinitum.*

Thus all Windows' files, in their kind, are bit by files that come behind.

Maximize the File Spy icon, read, and weep, for this is the way of the future.

WINFILE SPY

When you launch the FileSpy "Sleuth" icon in Windows, it creates the WinFile Spy window. This window will, thereafter, list all file activity during your Windows session. The information recorded includes the name of each file accessed, the directory where it can be found, and the time and date the file was accessed.

Minimize the window, and the WinFile Spy icon will display the name of each file, one file at a time, as Windows accesses it. If left active, the WinFile Spy icon will also follow you into any Windows applications that you use, recording each file that your application uses. You can open the WinFile Spy window at any time, even from another Windows application, to view a complete record of all files that have been accessed since you launched FileSpy for Windows.

Note: Data are not written to disk by FileSpy, so if you close WinFile Spy or exit Windows, the file access information it has recorded will be erased. You can, however, escape to DOS through a hot-key such as DosGate without disrupting WinFile Spy. WinFile Spy will not record your DOS session, though.

DOS FILESPY

For that, you need the DOS version of FileSpy. Fortunately, this is also part of the FileSpy program that you installed on your hard drive from the utility disk that came with this book. Once you add the FileSpy activation line (`HISPY.SYS`) to your `CONFIG.SYS` file (see the "Installation" section in this book), FileSpy will be memory resident in DOS and will be activated each time you boot up your PC. So whenever you exit Windows or escape to DOS from Windows, DOS FileSpy will be running.

Note: A Hard Impact device driver screen will pop up briefly on your screen whenever you turn on your PC. FileSpy is a subset of Hard Impact, a commercial software package, as explained later in this chapter, and it makes use of the Hard Impact device driver. You invoke this device driver with the "HISPY.SYS" line you added to your `CONFIG.SYS` file. The device driver is used by both WinFile Spy and FileSpy for DOS.

Like WinFile Spy, DOS FileSpy presents you with a filename each time the system accesses a file. The filenames are displayed one at a time in the upper-right corner of your DOS screen. Unlike WinFile Spy, DOS FileSpy does not give you a cumulative record of all files accessed during your DOS session.

While in DOS, you can toggle DOS FileSpy off by changing to the directory containing FileSpy (this should be `C:\MTOOLS`, unless you changed the drive or directory during the installation of the utilities). There type "HIDOS OFF" to deactivate DOS FileSpy. Type "HIDOS ON" in that same directory to toggle DOS FileSpy back on. You can also include this toggle in your `PATH` statement in your `AUTOEXEC.BAT` file, so that you can activate it whatever directory you may be in.

HARD IMPACT

As mentioned earlier, FileSpy is an introductory subset of Hard Impact, commercial software for monitoring disk utility. Hard Impact provides a graphical user interface (GUI) that illustrates file activity and permits you to compress files, delete unnecessary ones, and improve system performance by organizing directories with the most frequently accessed files at the top of the directories.

Hard Impact is what graphical user interfaces are all about—being graphic (Figure 12.7).

You pick a directory and Hard Impact lists files and graphs access activity by the amount of disk space (pie chart) and number of files (bar chart) in each category. You can see *exactly* what you use and what you do not and the impact on disk storage.

Hard Impact takes the guesswork out of freeing disk space. It monitors and summarizes file access, then graphs the results. You can select groups of inactive or rarely used files to be compressed with the press of a button and sent into EXILE, a special directory from whence they can easily be retrieved. The result is megabytes of precious free disk space, and no more archiving or erasing by guess and by golly.

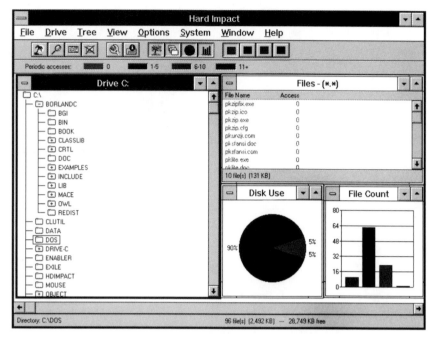

Figure 12.7   The commercial release of Hard Impact

For those of you with sophisticated technical concerns, Hard Impact uses software licensed from PK Ware to do the compression, so the shrunken files are both visible inside the directory and easily decompressed or attended to with the popular PK UnZip and associated software.

Those of you who can't abide secrets, turn on FileSpy, which prints the filename being accessed up in the title bar (or the top of the screen under DOS). It's instructive to see how much file activity Windows and its applications engage in. You'll see why a disk cache is essential, and why Windows can be such a performance dog.

Hard Impact is a solid hit. So solid, in fact, that we talked the developer out of the FileSpy portion to include with the tools disk that accompanies this book. To order the complete commercial release of Hard Impact, call 1-800-453-7849. The price is $59.95, plus $1.50 for shipping and handling.

The software programs contained on this disk are not in the public domain. NoFrag, MapDrive, DosGate, TmpErase, and FileFind are Copyright 1993, Paul Mace. You may not duplicate or distribute these programs without the author's permission, except for archival purposes. The underlying technology of NoFrag and MapDrive is patent pending. FileSpy is Copyright 1993, Software Workshop Inc.

Index

Paul Mace's Tools for Windows
System Requirements and
Installation Instructions

System Requirements

To install and use Tools for Windows, you must have:

- 386SX processor or greater
- 2 MB RAM or greater
- 1500K hard disk space
- Windows 3.1.

Installation

Place the distribution diskette in a drive (for instance, `A:`). In Windows choose `File|Run` and type `A:\SETUP.EXE` at the command line. Or in File Manager, select the drive the diskette is in and double-click on `SETUP.EXE`.

To run FileSpy, you must also place the line:

```
DEVICE=C: \MTOOLS\HISPY.SYS
```

in your DOS `CONFIG.SYS` file, and you must reboot your PC.